The Victor KNOW & BELIEVE Series

This book is part of The Victor KNOW & BELIEVE Series, an eight-volume library of the major doctrines of the Bible all of which are written in a clear, down-to-earth style. Other books in the series are:

Editor of the Series is Bruce L. Shelley, Ph.D., professor of Church History, Conservative Baptist Theological Seminary, Denver, Colorado.

VICTOR Know and Believe SERIES

The Bible: Breathed From God

Robert L. Saucy, Th.D.

Edited by Bruce L. Shelley, Ph.D.

This book is designed for your personal reading pleasure and profit. It is also designed for group study. A Leader's Guide with helps and hints for teachers is available from your local Christian bookstore or from the publisher at $2.25.

VICTOR BOOKS

a division of SP Publications, Inc., Wheaton, Illinois
Offices also in Fullerton, California • Whitby, Ontario, Canada • London, England

Dewey Decimal Classification: 220
   Subject Headings: HOLY SCRIPTURES;
   SCRIPTURES, HOLY

Library of Congress Catalog Card Number: 78-056740
ISBN: 0-88207-778-3

VICTOR BOOKS
a division of SP Publications, Inc.
P.O. Box 1825 ● Wheaton, Illinois 60187

CONTENTS

Introduction

Signs of evangelical vitality are all around us. Prominent personalities from politics, sports, and entertainment have recently "come out" for Christ. Publication houses report record sales of evangelical titles. Large conventions of evangelical believers catch the eye of the national wire services and the major magazines. The public is discovering the meaning of "born again."

This rather sudden exposure in the secular press has a happy side and a sad side. The happy side is the opportunity for millions of Americans to encounter the Gospel of Jesus Christ. For a half-century biblical Christianity has received mostly scorn from the spokesmen of American culture—movies, newspapers, novels, and television. The public was so busy laughing at the Gospel that it couldn't listen to it. Today, some are listening.

The sad side of this exposure is the evident weakness of "born again" religion. The major polls reveal that it is largely experience-centered, and almost any weird brush with mystery seems to do.

Biblical Christianity has an experiential element, but it is linked with doctrine and Body. It is what we think and to what we belong as well as what we experience.

That is where this book and others in the Victor Know and Believe Series come in. These eight books, designed for personal or group studies, aim at adding truth to testimony. As evangelicals, we should not only speak up in American society; may we say something when we do.

Bruce L. Shelley
Editor

1

The Revelation of God

Though some deny it, man is a religious creature. His heart and mind raise questions that his surroundings cannot answer. Where did I come from? Where am I going? What is the purpose of my being here? What is the reason for life and history? Without an authoritative revelation, these questions must remain unanswered.

Two conditions make an authoritative revelation necessary. First, man's limitations make it impossible for him to find answers to his persistent questions. To know his origin, man must have been there. But he obviously could not have witnessed his own creation.

Moreover, to know the meaning and purpose of life he must be able to grasp the whole of history. But each person fills only an infinitesimal spot in the stream of time. We are like marchers in a long parade. We may be able to view and understand something of the participants around us, but unless someone gives us the pattern of the entire parade, we have no idea what the whole show looks like or what its final destination is. Someone observed that there are few things reason can discover with so much certainty and ease as its own insufficiency.

A second condition making revelation necessary is the fallen state of man's reason. Man's understanding is not only limited in scope; it is by nature hindered by sin. While all men do not accept the biblical concept of *sin,* thinkers of all ages have recognized a disturbance that keeps man from perceiving correctly even his own limited life on earth. Shakespeare once said, "Now see that noble and most sovereign reason, like sweet bells jangled, out of tune and harsh." The Scriptures describe men separated from God in sin as "darkened in their understanding" and "futile in their speculations" (Eph. 4:18; Rom. 1:21). Psychologists describe man as a rationalizing animal. By this they mean that our reason is in league with our will. We cannot act and live one way and think and reason another. Our reason will inevitably seek to justify our actions. Thus man, whose will shuns the right, ends up with his reason distorting the truth.

Pythagoras, a Greek philospher and mathematician of the sixth century B.C., saw clearly the plight of all men. "It is not easy," he said, "to know [duties], except men were taught them by God himself, or by some person who has received them from God, or obtained the knowledge of them through some divine means." Reason is like a mirror. It can shine truthfully on the great questions of life only as it reflects the light of divine revelation imparted to it from God.

The Possibility of God's Revelation

If we grant, then, that those ultimate questions that surround our existence will remain unanswered except for a supernatural revelation, is such a revelation possible? Our reasons for expecting such a revelation lie in the nature of man and the nature of God.

Contrary to all other creatures, man is not satisfied with only his earthly environment. His nature reveals an incompleteness, a searching and longing for something more. Physically he is a part of nature, but spiritually he transcends nature, searching for something nature cannot supply. The logic of the laws of want and supply would argue for some realm to answer these needs.

Certainly, one would expect a Creator to structure reality suitable for the needs of every creature. Even naturalistic evolution argues for the adaptability of everything to its environment. Something in the environment of every creature sustains it or else it dies and ceases to exist. The enduring questions of the human mind about the supernatural argue—even on the evolutionary principle—that a transcendent realm exists and answers back to man. Otherwise the ability of man to raise these questions should have ceased long ago. In fact, this evolutionary principle refutes a natural evolutionary process which explains man as the mere product of chance happenings of nature. Such an explanation does not account for the rise of human questions beyond nature or for their sustained existence. We must conclude, therefore, that it is reasonable to expect a revelation to answer the need of man's nature.

Turning to the nature of God, we find that it is likewise reasonable to expect Him to disclose Himself to man. Every intelligent being we know desires to communicate with others and make himself known. It is reasonable, therefore, to presume that a personal God would desire to communicate Himself. This is all the more plausible when we consider the biblical teaching that man is made in the image of God and desires fellowship with God. Surely a God of love would respond to the need of His creatures, especially a need He planted within them.

If we grant, then, that a revelation from God is what we would expect from God—given the natures of man and God—is such a revelation possible? Can a God who is outside of this world and infinite in His person, communicate with man who is but a finite creature?

Some men have argued that we can only know a being who corresponds to our nature and therefore we cannot know God who is so completely different. We must agree that the God of the Bible is presented as the incomparable One. Through the prophet Isaiah God declared, "To whom then will you liken Me that I should be his equal?" (40:25) But in all of His infinite difference, He is also revealed as the God who made man in His image and likeness (Gen. 1:26). Included in this divine likeness in man is the capacity for personal communication. Surely this gift would find its first use in communicating with the Creator. To exalt the greatness of God and then limit His ability to make a creature with whom He can communicate is quite absurd. The One who gave us eyes to see, ears to hear, and a mind to understand can certainly use these same faculties in making Himself known to man.

The Means of God's Revelation

Since God is the God of the entire universe, being its Creator and

Sustainer, it is only natural that witness to Him be seen in all things. Thus, the Bible depicts the revelation of God through many avenues. In the classification of these forms two great categories are usually noted: (1) general revelation and (2) special revelation. By *general revelation* is meant that revelation which is addressed to, and therefore available to, all men at all times. *Special revelation,* on the other hand, is that revelation which God has given at special times to particular people. These categories are sometimes labelled "natural" and "supernatural" revelation. The distinction suggests that general revelation is communicated through the media of natural phenomena while special revelation is made through an intervention in the natural. A further difference rests in the purpose of each type of revelation. Berkhof, the late theologian, explained:

> General revelation is rooted in creation, is addressed to man as man, and more particularly to human reason, and finds its purpose in the realization of the end of his creation, to know God and thus enjoy communion with Him. Special revelation is rooted in the redemptive plan of God, is addressed to man as sinner, can be properly understood and appropriated only by faith, and serves the purpose of securing the end for which man was created in spite of the disturbance wrought by sin (Louis Berkhof, *Systematic Theology.* Grand Rapids: Wm. B. Eerdmans, 1941, p. 37).

General Revelation

1. The forms of general revelation. As we indicated earlier, God reveals Himself through all of His created works. This revelation, available to all, may be seen through two primary forms, the nature of the universe and the nature of man himself.

Longfellow wrote, "Nature is a revelation of God; art a revelation of man." Even as the works of man reveal his abilities and powers, so the universe displays characteristics of God. The psalmist declared, "The heavens are telling of the glory of God and the firmament is declaring the work of His hands" (Ps. 19:1). The glory of God refers to the very nature of God made manifest. It is the display of His attributes or characteristics.

In his letter to the Romans, Paul told which characteristics of God are revealed through nature. Speaking of people who have not received any special revelation, the Apostle wrote, "that which is known about God is evident within them; for God made it evident to them. For since the creation of the world His invisible attributes, His eternal power and divine nature, have been clearly seen, being understood through what has been made, so that they are without excuse. For even though they knew God, they did not honor Him as God, or give thanks" (Rom. 1:19-21). Thus, in creation God reveals His "eternal power" and "divine nature." This "nature" refers to those qualities which show Him to be God and worthy of worship. Though He is not part of nature as some religions affirm, and though He is invisible and cannot be seen with the natural eye, God is nevertheless disclosed in His handiwork, which bears His marks so that no man can escape the fact of His existence.

Author and speaker Richard Wurmbrand relates the story of a Russian couple who were both sculptors but who had been taught all of their lives that there was no God:

Once, we worked on a statue of Stalin. During the work, my wife asked me: "Husband, how about the thumb? If we could not oppose the thumb to the other fingers—if the fingers of the hands were like toes—we could not hold a hammer, a mallet, any tool, a book, a piece of bread. Human life would be impossible without this little thumb. Now, who has made the thumb? We both learned Marxism in school and know that heaven and earth exist by themselves. They are not created by God. So I have learned and so I believe. But if God did not create heaven and earth, if he created only the thumb, he would be praiseworthy for this little thing.

"We praise Edison and Bell and Stephenson who have invented the electric bulb, the telephone and the railway and other things. But why should we not praise the one who has invented the thumb? If Edison had not had a thumb he would have invented nothing. It is only right to worship God who has made the thumb."

The husband became very angry . . . "Don't speak stupidities! You have learned that there is no God. And you can never know if the house is not bugged and if we will not fall into trouble. Get into your mind *once and for all* that there is no God. In heaven there is *nobody!*"

She replied: "This is an even greater wonder. If in heaven there were the Almighty God in whom in stupidity our forefathers believed, it would be only natural that we should have thumbs. An Almighty God can do everything, so he can make a thumb, too. But if in heaven there is nobody, I, from my side, am decided to worship from all my heart the 'Nobody' who has made the thumb." (Richard Wurmbrand, *Tortured for Christ*. London: Hodder and Stoughton, 1967, p. 23.)

Not only the existence of nature about us, but also its ongoing processes which sustain life and activity, evidence the presence of God. The Lord "did not leave Himself without witness, in that He did good and gave you rains from heaven and fruitful seasons, satisfying your hearts with good and gladness" (Acts 14:17). We commonly refer to catastrophes as "acts of God," but the Apostle declares that the normal beneficial workings of nature we so often take for granted as natural laws are direct evidence of the reality of God. Jesus, for example, saw the hand of God feeding the birds of the air and clothing the lilies and grass of the field (Matt. 6:26-30).

When we turn from viewing the universe around us and look directly at ourselves we also see evidence of God. This evidence comes from the total personality of man, but especially from his moral nature. Speaking to the Athenians who worshipped "an unknown God," Paul argued against the worship of all human crafted idols by pointing to our own human nature: "in Him we live and move and exist, as even some of your poets have said, 'For we also are His offspring.' Being then the offspring of God, we ought not to think that the Divine Nature is like gold or silver or stone, an image formed by the art and thought of man" (Acts 17:28-29). In other words, he said, if we are the creatures of God, He is at least as great as we are and that means that He is a living Person.

Centuries before Paul, the prophet Isaiah used the same reasoning against people who thought that they could perform their evil practices unnoticed. "You turn things around! Shall the potter be considered as equal with the clay . . .? Or what is formed say to him who formed it, 'He has no understanding'?" (Isa. 29:16) The abilities of man and his accomplishments are intended to point beyond themselves to an even greater Creator, God.

The height of God's revelation through natural channels comes in the conscience or moral nature of man. Here we not only see God as the powerful Creator, but as the moral Lawgiver and Judge. The nature and history of man reveal a sense of right and wrong within him. Paul declared, "For when Gentiles who do not have the Law [written] do instinctively the things of the Law, these, not having the Law are a law to themselves, in that they show the work of the Law written in their hearts, their conscience bearing witness, and their thoughts alternately accusing or else defending themselves" (Rom. 2:14-15).

The Apostle stated further that we use this knowledge of right and wrong to judge others, but unfortunately it does not have power to make us perform the right. He concluded, "Therefore you are without excuse, every man of you who passes judgment, for in that you judge another, you condemn yourself; for you who judge practice the same things" (Rom. 2:1).

This sense of "oughtness" led the German philosopher Immanuel Kant to a belief in a God—even though he rejected the authority of the Scriptures. In a similar way, C.S. Lewis, the English literary scholar and perhaps the most popular apologist for Christianity in recent times, testified that the evidence for a moral law outside of man freed him from atheism.

Some social scientists object that the moral laws by which we seek to operate through our consciences are only the product of our society. They are placed there by our educational environment. While it is true that we may have learned some of the rules of acceptable behavior from our parents or others, this does not prove that the reality of these rules is the product of our teachers any more than the reality of the multiplication tables, which we also learned through education, is the product of our teachers.

Furthermore, while there are considerable differences in moral codes between societies, there are amazing similarities at the fundamental levels. We have often heard that in some cultures the thief or treacherous person is highly regarded while in others he is considered an outcast. The real test of our moral sense, however, is not in what we prize in actions toward others. The true revelation of our rule of right and wrong comes in what we prize in relation to ourselves. A thief may be highly honored among his people when he steals from others, but he does not approve of stealing when it is against himself. Likewise, it may be honorable among some people to kill others, but is there anyone who feels that it is a good thing to have his closest friend killed or be killed himself?

Contrary to this popular objection, the sense of right and wrong and the uneasy feeling that comes when we have violated some standard is witness to all men of a moral God. "The sense within me that I owe a debt," Robert Browning wrote, "assures me—somewhere must be Somebody, ready to take his due. All comes to this: where due is, there acceptance follows. Find Him who accepts the due."

2. *The effect of general revelation.* We have seen that through general revelation God makes Himself known as God. He reveals His creative power and those fundamental characteristics which mark Him as God before whom all men should bow in submission. In addition, He shows all men that He is a moral God who demands justice and will one day judge the world by His standard.

God's purpose in making Himself known in these ways to all men is that they might recognize His work and seek Him. Desiring to preach to the Athenians the true God, the Apostle Paul pointed to the works of God as Creator (Acts 17:24), as Sustainer of all life (v. 25) and as the Ruler of history (v. 26). God performs these works, the Apostle said, in order that men "should seek God, if perhaps they might grope for Him and find Him, though He is not far from each one of us" (v. 27).

This purpose of general revelation, however, is thwarted by sin. In the passage where Paul asserted that men know God (Rom. 1:18-23), he also declared that they "suppress the truth in unrighteousness" (v. 18). "For even though they knew God, they did not honor Him as God, or give thanks; but they became futile in their speculations, and their foolish heart was darkened" (v. 21). According to the Apostle, men cannot help but know about God, but they try to silence His voice, substituting their own philosophy and man-centered thoughts. "They exchanged the truth of God for a lie, and worshiped and served the creature rather than the Creator" (Rom. 1:25).

The problem, however, is not fundamentally one of the intellect, but a problem of the will. Ever since the entrance of sin into the world through the temptation to be like God (Gen. 3:5), man has refused to surrender to the only true God. He chooses to live an ego-centered, rather than a God-centered, life. From this improper and perverted base, man seeks to construct a satisfying philosophy of life. But he never attains the truth, because he gives his own meaning to the data of general revelation rather than acknowledging God and seeking to understand all things from His perspective. God says, in "professing to be wise, they became fools" (Rom. 1:22).

Despite man's failure to hear the voice of God or to see His hand in general revelation, such a revelation retains one benefit. Because all men do, in fact, have the sense of the divine, it renders them inexcusable before God. Paul says that the display of God in creation renders men "without excuse" (Rom. 1:20). They ought to see God, but they do not because they will not.

This inexcusable position is made even more plain in the fact that all men judge others by their innate sense of right and wrong. If God would simply turn in their direction the statements they use to accuse others, they would clearly indict themselves for their failure to live according to what they know is right. While general revelation does not solve the problem of sin, it does point out the need of salvation.

In addition to rendering all men without excuse, general revelation contributes to the preservation of human society and culture. Thanks to general revelation, some religious and ethical concepts prevail in almost every society. The ideas of truth and falsehood, justice and injustice, which help to maintain order among peoples, likewise trace their source to this revelation. In short, general revelation helps to check the tendency of sin to create chaos and degeneration. Left alone, human nature would soon bring to an end human history and civilization.

Finally, general revelation has a practical effect in evangelism. The Apostle Paul recognized that all men were aware of God. The altar to an unknown god gave evidence of that fact (Acts 17:23). So Paul used this awareness of God which comes through general revelation as a point of contact with the Athenians and pointed them to the knowledge of the true God found in Jesus Christ: "He will judge the world in righteousness through a Man whom He has appointed" (Acts 17:30-31).

The Need for Special Revelation

While the disclosure of God in the universe and in the nature of man reveals God, it was never designed to supply all that God wanted man to know about Himself and of His will for man. God made man for Himself. He created Him for fellowship with his Maker. Surrounded by the beauty of the Garden of Eden, Adam and Eve could know the handiwork of God, but to know God personally they needed direct communication. From the beginning, therefore, God not only revealed Himself through His creation, but directly through words.

Through words, man learned the will of God for his life. Gazing at creation and reflecting on his own nature could never give to Adam specific instructions about the care of the Garden (Gen. 2:15) or God's broader purpose for the ruling of the earth (Gen. 1:26-28). To test his obedience, God also communicated His will about the tree of the knowledge of good and evil (Gen. 2:16-17). Thus, from the beginning general revelation through nature provided only the background for personal verbal communication.

The great need of man, since the entrance of sin into the world, is a way of salvation. It is here that the inadequacy of general revelation looms greatest. Through nature and conscience, history reveals that men have come to realize that there is a God and that He has established the world on the principles of moral law. There is also the consciousness that no one is able to live up to this law consistently. But nowhere in nature or the constitution of man do we find a way out of this dilemma.

The history of religions reveals that when people do not receive the special revelation of God they find no true release from guilt. Religions are established in search of answers, but apart from the special revelation brought through Christ, religious men remain trapped within the knowledge they have through general revelation. They know they ought to live up to certain standards, but they don't. Consequently, they establish ways to compensate for their failure.

Inevitably, religions founded on general revelation are religions of works. Being without true salvation, they only increase obligation. Without the special revelation of God's forgiveness through Christ, we have no rest from the burden of guilt. To the psalmist, "the heavens are telling of the glory of God" (Ps. 19:1), but "the law of the Lord is perfect, restoring the soul" (v. 7).

Since the Fall of man, special revelation not only adds certain truths lacking in the revelation of God in creation; it also speaks to man's tendency to reject what is revealed to him through general revelation. Until he is brought back to God through a personal relationship with Jesus Christ he cannot view the universe around him from God's perspective. Only the illuminating work of God can open eyes blinded by sin. The pious psalmist is the individual who sees the glory of God in the heavens (Ps. 19:1). The atheistic astronomer views the same heavens and comes to a different conclusion. John Calvin, French theologian and reformer, aptly illustrated the necessity of special revelation for man to read the "book of nature" correctly. He noted:

Just as old or bleary-eyed men and those with weak vision, if you thrust before them a most beautiful volume, even if they recognize it to be some sort of writing, yet can scarcely construe two words, but with the aid of spectacles will begin to read distinctly; so Scripture, gathering up the otherwise confused knowledge of God in our minds, having dispersed our dullness, clearly shows us the true God (Calvin: *Institutes of the Christian Religion*, Philadelphia: The Westminster Press, 1960, 1, vi, 1).

Special revelation compliments general revelation so that together they provide man with the knowledge of God that undergirds all of life. The Lord speaks His Word to the special situations, communing in personal fellowship to meet individual needs. But such intervention would lack meaning, if the universe in all of its routine and natural processes were not also viewed as the work of His hand and under His sovereign Lordship.

2

God's Special Revelation

Man's knowledge of God is due solely to God's gracious revelation of Himself. Unless God shows Himself, man gropes in darkness forever. But God has revealed Himself in the created works of His hands. Moreover, the Bible declares that He has disclosed Himself in a more direct and personal way to His people throughout history. The nature and means of this revelation, however, have sparked considerable controversy.

Some theologians tell us that God has revealed Himself in His mighty acts throughout history, but not in words. Others point to the personal revelation of God in Christ, not to His acts. Since the Bible calls Christ the Word of God (John 1:1), these men argue that the words of the Bible cannot be the Word of God. Surely, they say, Christ is much more than mere words written by men. These conflicting teachings in the church today demand that we direct our attention to what the Scriptures say about God's special revelation.

The Various Methods of Revelation

The writer of Hebrews summarized nicely the main course of special revelation when he declared, "God, after He spoke long ago to the fathers in the prophets in many portions and in many ways, in these last days has spoken to us in His Son" (Heb. 1:1-2).

20

This statement tells us that there has been a history of special revelation and that it includes a variety of methods climaxing in the coming of the Son of God.

We may note here the principal methods of this revelation.

1. Theophanies. The word "theophany" comes from two Greek words, *theos* meaning "God" and *phaino* meaning "to make visible" or "to appear." A theophany is therefore an appearance of God. This manner of revelation was prominent during the early portions of the Bible.

In making Himself visible, God took several forms. On one occasion, Abraham welcomed three men into his tent to show them hospitality. Two of them were angels, but the third was the Lord Himself (Gen. 18:22; 19:1; see also the man who wrestled with Jacob, Gen. 32:24, 30). On another occasion, God spoke to Moses out of a bush which was burning, but not being consumed. Many times the Scriptures just tell us that God appeared to certain people (see Gen. 12:7; 17:1; 26:2).

Often, however, God appeared as the Angel of the Lord. Several statements make it clear that this person was more than an ordinary angel. He declared to Jacob that He was God (Gen. 31:11-13), and was clearly identified as God on other occasions (Gen. 16:13; Judges 13:21-22). Since we are told in the New Testament that the Son is the revealer of God (John 1:18), and this special angel never appears again after the coming of Christ, many Bible students believe that the Angel was none other than the Son Himself before He took on Himself human nature at Bethlehem.

In one sense, the coming of Christ in human flesh was also a theophany, but it is different than all the rest. In all of the others God simply assumed a form; in the birth of Jesus, God the Son took on Himself a genuine human nature.

2. Dreams and visions. Although dreams do not play a major role in revelation, they are used in significant instances to convey God's Word, especially in the Books of Genesis and Daniel. Well-known cases include Jacob's dream of a ladder extending from earth to heaven (Gen. 28:12-16) and the dreams of Joseph concerning his exaltation above his brothers (Gen. 37:5-7, 9). Solomon (1 Kings 3:5 ff.) and Joseph, the husband of Mary (Matt. 1:20; 2:13, 19), were also given revelations in dreams.

Nor were dreams limited to God's people. Pharaoh and Nebuchadnezzar had dreams concerning significant events affecting the future course of history (Gen. 41:1 ff.; Dan. 2:3 ff.). In both cases, however, the interpretations were conveyed through those who belonged to God's people.

Closely associated with dreams but much more common as a means of revelation were visions. The writings of the prophets are full of accounts of the reception of visions from God. While in some instances what was seen was described in a pictorial scene, in others the object of the vision was words. Ezekiel clearly saw the temple in Jerusalem in a vision (Ezek. 8:3) while the prophet Amos spoke of "the words . . . which he saw concerning Israel" (Amos 1:1, KJV). Prophets were, in fact, sometimes called "seers" indicative of the truth that revelation was somehow conceived visually, exactly how we do not know. Perhaps it was simply a divine presentation in the mind of the recipient for which he was given understanding.

3. Direct communication. Frequently, we find that God simply spoke directly to people. "God said," "the Word of the Lord came unto me," and "thus saith the Lord" are expressions occurring over and over. Again, we do not fully understand the means of this type of communication. It seems to have varied. In some instances there appears to have been an audible sound, as in the case of Paul hearing the voice from heaven (Acts 9:4) and possibly Samuel (1 Sam. 3:1 ff.). At other times it must have been some type of inward speech such as we may use in silent prayer to God. When the Holy Spirit told Peter that three men were looking for him (Acts 10:19) or directed the church to send out Barnabas and Saul (Acts 13:2), it was undoubtedly this type of speaking. The disclosure must have been similar when Paul received revelation from Christ in the Arabian desert (Gal. 1:11-17).

A unique direct communication was given to Moses. Exodus 33:11 states, "Thus the Lord used to speak to Moses face to face, just as a man speaks to a friend." When Miriam and Aaron questioned the authority of Moses, God affirmed the unique place of Moses. To the prophets of that time He revealed Himself through dreams and visions, but with Moses, He communed "mouth to mouth" (Num. 12:6-8).

4. Angels. Occasionally, we find God using angels in the communication of His revelation. They appear in this role especially at the beginning of a new work of God. For example, the Law was given to Moses through the mediation of angels (Gal. 3:19; Acts 7:53). An angel also announced the good news of the birth of the Saviour to the shepherds outside of Bethlehem (Luke 2:10, 13). One of the most interesting examples of revelation through an angel occurred with Daniel. On two occasions God answered his prayer for Israel by sending a message through angels, one of whom is identified as Gabriel (Dan. 9:20-21; 10:10-21). While angels are superior to men in many ways, it is clear that they are only messengers and not originators of the Word. Peter declared that even angels "long to look" into the good news of the Gospel (1 Peter 1:12).

5. Miracles. Throughout the time when God was communicating His Word directly to man, He often gave evidence of His presence by performing miracles. By a miracle, we are referring to an act that is radically different from ordinary events. Normally, God operates His universe according to what are known as natural laws. A miracle occurs when God chooses to act in an extraordinary way for the purpose of revealing Himself.

The biblical language for miracles reveals their revelatory function. Speaking of the miracles of Jesus, Peter described them as "miracles and wonders and signs" (Acts 2:22). This is not a reference to three different kinds of acts, but the same act from three viewpoints. The first term, "miracle," looks at the deed from the vantage of the power displayed. The Greek word used is *dunamis* from which we derive our word dynamite. From the perspective of their striking character and the amazement evoked, they are "wonders." The last word, "signs," points directly to their purpose as revelatory events. Signs in Scripture are like pointers which direct our attention to something.

According to the prophecies, the Messiah would come and work miracles as signs pointing to His Messiahship. For this reason the Jews continually asked Jesus, "What sign do You show to us?" (John 2:18; Matt. 12.38; 16:1) The miracle of the healing of the paralytic (Mark 2) illustrates these three dimensions of a miracle. Clearly, the dynamic power was displayed when the man lying on the pallet got up and walked (v. 12). The effect of wonder is seen in the statement that "they were all amazed and were glorifying God, saying, 'We have never seen anything like this'" (v. 12). But the ultimate point of the miracle was stated by Jesus: "that you may know that the Son of Man has authority on earth to forgive sins" (v. 10). Such authority naturally belongs to God. Thus, the miracle was a revelation of the deity of our Lord.

Miracles are involved in revelation in two important ways. First, they point to the fact that revelation is happening. They make us sit up and take notice that God is at work. Second, they reveal something of the nature of God's power and the purpose for which He exerts it. Although in some cases it may be difficult to see anything more than the evidence of God's power over nature—as in the story of Jesus turning water into wine (John 2) —most instances reveal God's power overcoming sin and its effects. The healing of the sick and lame, and the restoration of sight to the blind all point to the triumph of God over the misery of sin. The raising of Lazarus and others who had died announces the fact that sin's ultimate power is broken, and death, the last enemy of man, is vanquished by the power of God.

While miracles are a form of revelation, their full significance is known only through the Word. Miracles are thus seen as signs pointing to messengers of the Word. As Peter wrote, miracles "attested" or "accredited" the person of Christ to the people. They validated His person and therefore also His words which declared God's will and purpose. The Apostle Paul likewise pointed to the miraculous works God performed through him as "signs of a true apostle" (2 Cor. 12:12). They were his credentials, which validated his words as from God.

6. *The Person of Christ.* The writer to the Hebrews declared that "in these last days God has spoken to us in His Son . . ." (Heb. 1:2). In this Word, the revelation of God reaches its climax. The "many portions" of God's speech which had previously been revealed through "many ways" were only fragments pointing to the coming of Him "in whom are hidden all the treasures of wisdom and knowledge" (Col. 2:3).

In the coming of Christ we gain additional knowledge of God as He reveals Himself in a different way. For Christ did not so much *make* a revelation of God as He *is* the revelation. He is God incarnate, that is, God in human flesh. It is one thing to receive much knowledge about a person, but this never compares with meeting the person himself.

In Jesus Christ the world was confronted by God Himself. John declared that, "no man has seen God at any time; the only begotten God . . . He has explained Him" (John 1:18). This must not be interpreted to mean that Jesus was simply a greater teacher of divine truth than all previous teachers. He "explained" God in the sense that to view Him was to see God, even as He told Philip, "He who has seen Me has seen the Father" (John 14:9). He could say this because "in Him all the fulness of Deity," was resident, or as one interpreter explains, "God in all His fulness" dwelt in bodily form (Col. 2:9).

The revelation of God in Christ was given through His teachings. He was recognized as *the* teacher sent from God (John 3:2) speaking the words of God as none had before. But in addition to words, God spoke in the total character and acts of Jesus. This Word climaxed in the acts of the cross and resurrection. At Calvary, God revealed His infinite love in the gift of His Son and also His infinite holiness and righteousness in His sacrifice for sin. The message of redemption was complete and the promise of eternal life confirmed when He raised His Son from the dead.

Jesus is not simply the climax of revelation; He is the theme of all revelation. Scripture testifies to Him (John 5:39), for the prophets before Him and the apostles afterward were inspired by the Holy Spirit, who is also the Spirit of Christ (1 Peter 1:11; Rev. 19:10).

7. *Inspiration.* One final form of revelation occurs in the written Scriptures. Much of the Bible is simply the written record of revelation which was given in many of the forms we have already noticed. Dreams and visions were recorded, and direct communication of God's words to the prophets was written down. There is, however, one additional form of revelation seen in the giving of the Scriptures. This has been described as "concursive inspiration." The nature of this type of revelation may be seen when we compare it to other forms. When God spoke directly to men they were conscious of His controlling influence. When dreams and visions occurred the individuals were basically passive recipients of the message of God. Most certainly, when God wrote the Ten Commandments with His finger on the tablets of stone,

Moses could do nothing but bring them to the people.

On the other hand, in contrast to these who were conscious of the overpowering influence of God giving His revelation to them, we find those such as the Apostle Paul speaking and writing the Word without such conscious influence. For instance, we do not find such statements as, "The word of the Lord came to me," or "thus says the Lord." Rather, the Spirit of God worked inwardly and through their own personalities to reveal truth. It is evident in Paul's writings that his own mind and emotions were totally involved as he spoke God's truth. Yet the Spirit of God controlled him so that what he spoke was exactly what God desired to say. We might say that in this form of revelation God and man were joined, more closely than in any way except the person of Christ. It is only natural that such revelation would occur primarily in New Testament times when God by His Spirit took up His residence in the very heart of man.

In noting that the concursive inspiration form of revelation occurs primarily in the New Testament, and considering the prominence of other forms at other times, we see that there is a fundamental progression in the type of revelation used throughout revelatory history. All of the methods other than the unique Person of Christ may be summed up in three basic forms— appearances of God, or theophanies; some type of direct communication or prophecy; and concursive inspirations.

While all of these forms are present in every age from Moses to Christ, theophanies are first prominent, then prophecy, and finally, inspiration. Looking at the nature of these forms we find an advancement from the visible and external to the internal, from that which stands apart to that which is intimately near. This clearly follows the progression of God's entire relationship with man. In the Garden of Eden, man was separated from God through sin. But in Christ God has brought man near, through the redemption of the cross, and will someday dwell fully with him: "the tabernacle of God is among men, and He shall dwell among them" (Rev. 21:3). Despite these differences in the forms and relationships, however, the Bible never makes any distinction as to the revelatory value of each form. All are equally the revelation of God.

Acts and Words

It is clear from our discussion of the various forms God used to communicate His special revelation to us, that He used both actions and words. In fact, all of the forms mentioned could be categorized under one or both of these headings.

Many theologians today, however, deny that God has actually communicated to men in words. They refer to the "mighty acts" of God in history, but refuse to accept that any words, including those of the Bible, are really the words of God. According to this view, God acted and then by the Spirit opened the eyes of certain observers to perceive something about God's character and will in these acts. But this opening of the eyes was not in any sense a direct revelation of truth from God to man.

We may take the crucifixion of Jesus as an example. To the Jew who had seen many such killings outside the walls of Jerusalem, the death of Jesus may have appeared like any other. But God enlightened the minds of certain chosen observers to see that He was doing something on the cross for the salvation of man. The statements of this interpreter, however, must not be considered words from God. They remain the fallible words of men.

One advocate of this position sums it up this way: "There is no such thing as revealed truth. There are truths of revelation, that is to say, propositions which express the results of correct thinking concerning revelation; but they are not themselves directly revealed."

This denial that the words of Scripture are in fact revealed by God, and the affirmation that in the final analysis they are simply enlightened human words allows the critical scholar to pass judgment on which words most accurately reflect the truth in God's action.

In response to this position, the Bible affirms again and again the fact that God spoke (Heb. 1:1). The prophets declared that they received the word of God. Often they prefaced their messages with "thus says the Lord." This would be untrue if, in fact, it were their own enlightened interpretation. Similarly, the Apostle Paul declared specifically that what he proclaimed was "the word of God's message" and not "the word of men" (1 Thes. 2:13).

Furthermore, the essence of true faith as modeled in Abraham was belief in the "word" of God. Several times, Scripture records the act of Abraham's faith by declaring that he "believed God, and it was reckoned to him as righteousness" (Rom. 4:3; Gal. 3:6; James 2:23; Gen. 15:6). He, along with the others, is listed as a champion of faith because he "obtained promises" and believed them (Heb. 11:33, 39).

Finally, what can we say about the words of the Son of God? He affirmed that His teaching was not His own, but had its source in heaven and was from the Father (e.g. John 7:16; 8:28). "I speak just as the Father has told Me" (John 12:50). If the words of Jesus are not revelation from God, it is difficult to understand what He means by such a statement.

When we think about the Bible's claim that God revealed truth through words, we realize that there is no other way by which we could know the meaning of the acts of God and His will for us. Many witnessed the Exodus out of Egypt, the Babylonian captivity of Israel, the death of Christ, and the empty tomb. But all did not see the same meaning in these acts. Unless the true interpretation is revealed by God, we can only make our judgments, but never know for sure.

The Bible declares that God gave us the meaning of His acts. Sometimes it was by prediction prior to the event. Such was the case of the coming of the Spirit at Pentecost, which had been taught by Christ before He ascended to heaven (Acts 1:5). Sometimes the meaning accompanied the happening, as with the angels from heaven at the birth of Jesus (Luke 2:8). At other times the interpretation followed the action. The message of the Apostles is nothing less than the full interpretation of the great events of the cross and resurrection of the Saviour.

One final word of a practical nature may also be added concerning the use of words in communication. While most people would choose deafness over blindness, in reality the blind suffer less emotional disturbance than do the deaf. The reason has to do with the importance of words for personal relationships. Bernard Ramm notes:

> The warm personal relationships of life are carried on by means of conversation, and the deaf man is largely severed from those relationships. The soundless world is far more

frustrating than the sightless world. Radio drama is entertaining but a television drama robbed of the sound track is drained of all meaning. *In life as in drama it is the word which carries the meaning; it is the word which is the element of cohesion; and it is the word which is the necessary presupposition for warm personal friendships* (B. Ramm, *Special Revelation and the Word of God.* Grand Rapids: Wm. Eerdmans, 1971), p. 77.

According to our Lord, the essence of our eternal life is the knowledge of God (John 17:3). The Greek word used for knowledge signifies a personal experiential relationship with the object known. If God has not communicated to us with words, not only has He disregarded the best means of personal communication with which He created us, but our personal relationship with Him is seriously limited.

The Personal Word and the Written Word

The famous Swiss theologian Karl Barth stated, "the equation, God's Word is God's Son, makes anything doctrinaire in regarding the Word of God radically impossible." In this statement he expressed another common objection to a verbal revelation from God. Arguing that the actual meeting of a person is more than words, this view declares that God has revealed Himself personally in Christ. He is the Word of God (John 1:1). To say that the words of the Bible are also the words of God is therefore impossible. In fact, those who do are often charged with giving the words of the Bible such an emphasis that they obscure a relationship with the Word Himself. In plain terms, they are charged with bibliolatry—the worship of the Bible instead of the worship of the Word, the Son of God.

We must admit that some people have focused on the written words of Scripture without going on to fellowship with the living Word of whom it speaks. This was the problem of many Jews who rejected Jesus. They studied the Scriptures intently believing them to give the way of life, but Jesus said, "It is these [Scriptures] that bear witness of Me; and you are unwilling to come to Me, that you may have life" (John 5:39-40). This same tragic error can be committed today even by so-called "Bible believing" people who know all about the truth but do not have a living relationship with

Him who is the truth. Jesus said, "He who does not honor the Son does not honor the Father who sent Him" (John 5:23).

But if this separation is wrong so is the opposite separation which is often proposed today. According to the Scriptures there can be no real separation between the written words and the personal Word. In our own communication with another person we find his words to be the way we get to know him. Only through his words do we come to know his inner thoughts and feelings. In a real sense a person's words are only an extension of himself as he seeks to bridge the distance between himself and another. So the living God who came to earth in the Person of the Son, Jesus Christ, reveals His heart and mind to man through the medium of language, the Word of God.

According to the Apostle Peter, it was the Spirit of Christ who was the ultimate Author of the words of the Old Testament (1 Peter 1:11). That same Spirit was promised by the Lord to continue His teachings by inspiring the writers of the New Testament (John 16:12-15). In short, the words of the Bible are the words of Christ. To disparage the written words is therefore to dishonor their Author. Because the Scriptures are the words of the personal Word, they bear His same divine characteristics. They are living (Heb. 4:12), true (Ps. 19:8; 119:42; John 17:17), and everlasting (Ps. 119:89).

3

The Uniqueness of the Bible

The Scriptures of the Old and New Testaments claim to be the special revelation from God. But do they bear out such a claim?

Many religious groups also maintain that their sacred texts are a revelation of God. For example, Muslims believe that their holy book, *The Koran*, is divinely inspired. They insist that the Archangle Gabriel revealed it to Muhammad. In a similar way, Mormons argue that Joseph Smith received a direct revelation from God engraved on golden plates which he translated and published as the *Book of Mormon*. Other religions also have their sacred scriptures which claim to be revelations from God.

In the midst of all of these appeals to revelation, we might hope that the true revelation of God would stand out. If we are to hear the voice of God, His Word should be manifestly unique. If we compare the Bible with the other claimants, that is exactly what we find. The Scriptures bear the marks of a supernatural book.

The Teachings of the Bible

When we encounter the central teachings of the Bible, we find that no man or group of men could be their author. Not only do the scope and grandeur of the message transcend human ability, but the essential truth is also contrary to human thought. The entire message of the Bible aptly illustrates God's statement through the prophet Isaiah: "For My thoughts are not your thoughts, neither are your ways My ways . . . for as the heavens are higher than the earth, so are My ways higher than your ways, and My thoughts than your thoughts" (55:8-9).

1. The concept of God. From beginning to end the Bible focuses on God. Its perspective appears in the declaration, "Thine, O Lord, is the greatness and the power and the glory and the victory and the majesty, indeed everything that is in the heavens and the earth; Thine is the dominion, O Lord, and Thou dost exalt Thyself as head over all" (1 Chron. 29:11). He is the all-pervading sovereign God who rules the universe, directing all things to their end for His glory.

Yet combined with this picture of His sovereign holiness is one of His infinite goodness, love, and mercy. "The Lord is good to all," the psalmist declares, "and His mercies are over all His works" (Ps. 145:9). Within His sovereign holiness and justice, He works out a plan of salvation in infinite love for sinful man.

The very nature of God is a mystery no human fully comprehends. Human history reveals belief in many gods (polytheism) or single unitarian gods. The Bible alone presents the unique God who is both one God and yet three personal manifestations—Father, Son, and Spirit. This trinitarian concept of God is not a contradiction to human reason as some charge. There is not one God and three Gods or one Person and three Persons. There is one divine Being who exists eternally in three modes or personal manifestations. While not an irrational contradiction to human minds, such a concept of God is not the invention of man, but the revelation of God.

2. The Concept of Christ. Likewise, no one like the Person of Christ is found in any other supposed revelation. Born of a virgin in the midst of humble surroundings, yet He was the eternal Son of God. Creator of all, yet He went to the cross to die at the hands of man. The British authority on comparative religions, J.N.D. Anderson, summarizes the unique place of the Christ of Scriptures among all human religions in this way:

> Other religions may, indeed, include the belief that God, or one of the gods, manifested himself once, or many times, in human form, or that some 'divine light-substance' has passed from one

individual to a succession of others. But Christianity alone has dared to claim that 'the one, omnipresent, omniscient Ground of all existence' has uniquely intervened in his creation, not by assuming the mere form or appearance of a man, but by actually becoming incarnate; not by living and teaching alone, but by actually dying a felon's death 'for us men and for our salvation'; and by putting his seal on the fact and efficacy of this intervention by rising again from the dead (J.N.D. Anderson, *Christianity and Comparative Religion,* Downers Grove, Ill., InterVarsity Press, 1970, p. 51).

Not only is Christ alone in His origin and the nature of His Person, but His life is without peer. He walked on earth in normal human situations yet claimed to be without sin (John 8:46). He never had to apologize or ask forgiveness for anything He did. Other religious leaders claimed to teach the way of life they had found. Christ claimed to be the Way of life (John 14:6). No other historical founder of a religion insisted that He was the one and only God.

Jesus' contemporaries testified that He spoke like no other man (John 7:46). Speaking with authority, He never asked for advice or permission. Yet in His moral perfection He never conveyed the impression of pride or sanctimonious aloofness.

Where did the Gospel writers get such a portrait of a person unless He was the unique revelation of God? The very restrained portrait of Him by the biblical writers testifies to their inspiration.

One has only to read the mythologies of various peoples to see the propensity of man to embellish the truth with fantastic imagination. Even the nonbiblical writings about Jesus, purporting to tell of His boyhood, portray Him as a childhood prodigy instructing His schoolteachers with hidden mysteries in the alphabet and astounding His family and playmates with miraculous works.

According to these apocryphal gospels, on one occasion at the age of five Jesus supposedly fashioned 12 sparrows out of clay on the Sabbath. When questioned by His father Joseph about such activity on the Holy Day, Jesus clapped his hands and the sparrows flew away chirping.

In total contrast, the Bible portrays the miracles of Christ with straightforward simplicity. Their purpose is not to amuse His audience or entertain the curious, but to demonstrate the glory of His Father in keeping with the total goal of His life.

The Biblical Account of Man

When we consider the biblical portrait of human beings we must ask, who would paint such a picture of man as we find in Scripture? Man's tendency is either to exalt himself above what he really is or to reduce himself below his true nature. The Dutch scholar Erasmus once said, "Man is to man either a god or a wolf."

On the one hand, human philosophies and theologies often extol the deity of man. The ancient Greek Heraclitus proclaimed, "The gods are immortal men, and men are mortal gods." Much later, German philosopher Georg Hegel announced the "implicit divinity" of all men and theologians spoke of that spark of deity in man which needs to be fanned into flames.

Under the more recent influence of naturalistic evolution, philosophers speak of man as the aristocrat of animals. According to psychologist B. F. Skinner, man is nothing more than a complex organism whose actions are controlled by his environment, much like Pavlov's dogs were trained to respond to certain stimuli.

The greatness of man—his freedom, his creativity, his ability to soar above the world by his spirit—and yet his bondage to the natural environment as a creature of earth, leave people perplexed about their own nature.

The Bible alone reveals man's true nature. The great questions all men ask—who am I? where did I come from? what is the purpose of my existence?—are all answered in the Scriptures. Man is a creature of earth (Gen. 2:7), but he is also formed in the image of God. He belongs to this world and therefore must labor to maintain the natural environment as his physical home. But he was also made for fellowship with God and therefore can never be satisfied by nature alone.

The problem of human identity stems not only from man's nature. It arises from sin. If man is in the image of God, why does he not act like God? Again the Bible provides the answer in a way that we would not expect from human writers. According to the Scriptures, man's dignity is marred by sin, sin for which man is responsible. To be sure, men recognize their failure to do what they ought. They confess their "inhumanity" against man. But without divine revelation men explain this flaw by some lack of knowledge or some evolutionary vestige of animal aggression. All such explanations sidestep full responsibility; they do not acknowledge the willful rebellion against God. Sin becomes the pitiful product of man's evolutionary environment, and so man becomes less than man.

The Bible, however, declares that man is a responsible sinner. It upholds the dignity of human freedom, the power to act, and the perversity of human conduct. Man is great, but fallen. The Scriptures, moreover, present the human condition in perfect candor. While they do not major on depravity, even the heroes of the faith cannot hide their weaknesses. Great men of faith are presented as sinners in need of God's salvation. Thus the biblical portrait of man is beyond human production.

The Biblical Concept of Salvation

When we consider the salvation revealed in the Scriptures, we see again evidence of uniqueness pointing to a divine source. The diverse means of salvation found in the world's religions boil down to one fundamental distinction. Salvation is either by human works or it is received by grace. The vast majority of religions fall into the first category, as illustrated in the following story about certain Hindus.

> We turned away from the river and came to an open stretch of land, a stony path between fields, hemmed in by low clay walls and thorny shrubs. It began to be hot. Every step kicked up dust. After a short while we came upon a young man, lying flat on the ground and apparently doing some gymnastic exercises. He got up, reached back with his left hand as far as he could, picked up a stone from a small heap lying there, stretched himself flat on the ground, reached with his right forward as far as possible and put the stone there on a similar small heap of stones . . . Dr. Govindam explained to me that the young man was not allowed to speak as long as he was occupied with this especially meritorious form of parikrama (circumambulation). On a particular spot of the parikrama

route, 108 pebbles had to be collected and then moved, as shown by the young man, pebble by pebble, the length of the body at a time. After all 108 pebbles have been moved the distance of about two steps, one starts all over again. How long does it take to make the pilgrimage in this manner? Weeks—perhaps months. We passed other devout people who had chosen this penance, among them an old widow. Dr. Govindam explained to us that she was probably doing it to gain merit that would profit her husband in the other world. . . . Weeks later I saw her still at it, a few kilometres ahead of the spot where we had first discovered her. She seemed so weak that after every twenty metres she remained lying exhausted next to her small pile of stones (K. Klostermaier, *Hindu and Christian in Vrindaban*, London: SCM Press, 1969, p. 20 ff).

Whether by the Hindu way of righteousness, the eightfold discipline of Buddhism's "Middle Way," or the fasting and prayer of Muslims, the majority of the nonbiblical religions seek to earn salvation by works. The naturalness of fallen man's approach to salvation is evident in the popular philosophy that entrance into heaven is gained by "doing the best I can."

Some religions, however, have their savior-gods who give salvation to those of faith. The most widely accepted form of Buddhism in Japan is based on the story of one named Amita who accumulated such a vast store of merit on his way to Buddhahood that he vowed to give rebirth in paradise to all who sincerely trusted in him and constantly repeated "Hail Amita-Buddha." Worshippers sing the hymn:

Have ye faith in Amita's Vow
Which takes us in eternally.
Because of Him, of His Great Grace
The Light Superb will all be thine.
(H.D. Lewis and R. L. Slater, *World Religions*, London: C. A. Watts, 1966, p. 78)

The concept of savior-gods was also widespread in ancient Egypt and Mesopotamia. But we must note that even in most beliefs in a god who saves, there is still the necessity of works to earn their favor. Moreover, they have no means of salvation which deals seriously with the obvious reality of human sin.

How different is the salvation of Scripture. The natural desire of man to earn merit is completely absent; all glory in salvation belongs to God. The historical reality of sin is fully upheld. Salvation is worked out by God's infinite love in a way that completely preserves His infinite holiness. Contrary to the mythical savior-gods of world religions, God's salvation is verifiably rooted in the historical death and resurrection of Jesus Christ. Such salvation is truly beyond the scope of human invention. The Apostle Paul, who had so earnestly walked the pharisaical road of human-works salvation, summed up in triumph the supernaturalness of God's salvation: "For God has shut up all in disobedience that He might show mercy to all. Oh, the depth of the riches both of the wisdom and knowledge of God! How unsearchable are His judgments and unfathomable His ways!" (Rom. 11:32-33)

The Evidence of Prophecy

Nowhere is the uniqueness of the Bible more evident than in the supernaturalness of its prophecies. Peoples, ancient and present, have always sought to know the events of the future. They have had their diviners, astrologers, and psychic fortune-tellers who pronounced what was going to take place. But in none of these is there any comparison with the prophecies of Scripture. Through the prophet Isaiah the God of the Bible challenges the false gods to declare the future. "Let them bring forth and declare to us what is going to take place . . . or announce to us what is coming. Declare the things that are going to come afterward, that we may know that you are gods" (Isa. 41:22-23). What the false gods were unable to do God claims to perform: "I declared the former things long ago" (Isa. 48:3).

To be sure, some outside of the Scriptures have been able to make amazing predictions beyond the ability of mere human guessing. But none compare with the prophets of Scripture. Some have predicted certain events in the near future which came true. But which prophet or group of prophets has ever predicted as numerous prophecies concerning nations, peoples, cities, and individuals as the Bible, some of which looked hundreds and even thousands of years into the future? Again, which prophet outside of the true prophets of Scripture has made predictions which to date have all been verified by history? The Scriptures are so bold as to label "false" every prophet whose predictions do not come to pass (Deut. 18:20-22). By this standard the Bible stands alone.

Illustrative of the prophetic themes of the Bible are the prophecies relating to the nation of Israel. A few of these, predicted in some cases hundreds of years before the fact, include oppression in another land (Egypt) for 400 years (Gen. 15:13-16), kings from Judah (Gen. 49:10), distinction from other peoples (Num. 23:9), dispersion and suffering because of unbelief (Deut. 28:64-67; Luke 21:20-24), continued preservation and final restoration (Amos 9:9-15; Rom. 11:25-29). These latter prophecies have yet to be completely fulfilled. But the absolutely unique historical event of 1948, the reestablishment of a nation after its people had been dispersed for centuries, points to the perfect fulfillment of all prophecies.

Even more than the prophecies of Israel are the predictions related to Christ, which are incredible apart from divine inspiration. From the details of the place of His birth in insignificant Bethlehem (Micah 5:2) to the casting of lots for His clothing at the foot of the cross (Ps. 22:14-18; Matt. 27:35), the events of His life were foretold hundreds of years prior to their occurrence. Some scholar concluded that a total of 333 prophecies concerning Christ have been fulfilled. The probability of that number of predictions concerning one single individual coming true by chance has been calculated as 1 out of 83 billion. With such odds, clearly these prophecies are not the product of human authorship alone. The God who knows the future and directs the course of history is the ultimate source.

Not only do the Bible's prophecies stand alone in their vastness and accuracy of fulfillment, but their purpose is also different than the divinations of men. Curiosity and the desire for power are the mainsprings of fortune-telling. But God discloses the future of nations and people for the purpose of revealing Himself and His will. Biblical prophecy is not designed to help God's people set dates, but to understand God and His plan for history that they might align their lives with Him and His purposes. Thus, prophecy marks the Bible as a unique writing.

The Unity of the Bible

Josh McDowell, a popular Christian speaker on university campuses, tells the story of encountering a representative of the *Great Books of the Western World*. This set includes the writing of many of the outstanding thinkers who shaped Western civilization, beginning with the ancient Greek philosophers and continuing down to recent times. Referring to these books, Josh challenged the representative to take just 10 of the authors, all from the same walk of life, the same time period, the same place, the same language, and pose to them one controversial subject. Would they agree? The gentleman paused for a moment and then replied, "No! You would have a conglomeration."

When we compare the obvious reality of this diversity of human thought with the unity found in the Bible, the evidence for its supernaturalness is overwhelming. Far from the similarities of the 10 authors mentioned above, the Bible is composed of the writings of over 40 men. From all walks of life, including kings, herdsmen, poets, philosophers, statesmen, legislators, fishermen, priests, and prophets, these men wrote over a time span of more than 1,500 years. They lived in diverse cultures, and wrote in a variety of literary styles. But the message of the Bible is one great drama in which all the parts fit together.

From "Paradise Lost" in Genesis to "Paradise Regained" in Revelation, the Bible presents the unfolding of God's great purpose for man which is worked out through His Son. Jesus Himself declared that the Scriptures bore witness of Him (John 5:39). In the Old Testament—as the hope of the world—and in the New—as the fulfillment of that hope—Christ and His work are the cord that ties all of the Scriptures together.

The Bible may be compared to the human body in which every part can only be explained in reference to the whole. So the great variety of the books of the Bible have their meaning only as they are parts of the Book. Such a work, encompassing the lives of generations of individuals, can only be accounted for by another Author, the Spirit of God, who is forever the same. The Psalmist wrote, "The sum of Thy Word is truth, And every one of Thy righteous ordinances is everlasting" (Ps. 119:160).

The Indestructibility of the Bible

Only an exceptional book stays around for 25 years. One that is read for a century is indeed very unusual, and those that last for more than a thousand years are extremely rare. Yet the Bible remains the most popular book in the world. This fact of enduring interest alone would point to something different about the Bible. Couple this with the determined efforts throughout history to attack and destroy the Scriptures and their unique character is plain.

Early in the life of the church, the Roman emperors tried to get rid of the Scriptures because they realized the life of the church was based on belief in them. In A.D. 303 Diocletian issued a royal edict demanding that every copy of the Bible be burned. He killed so many Christians and destroyed so many Bibles that he was confident he had brought Christianity to an end. Celebrating his triumph he had a coin struck with the inscription: "The Christian religion is destroyed and the worship of the gods restored." How wrong he was is evident in the fact that 10 years later the Roman Emperor Constantine converted to Christianity and a short time later commissioned Eusebius to prepare 50 copies of the Bible at government expense.

In more recent times, the Scriptures came under the vicious attack of "enlightened" skeptical and atheistic philosophers, but with the same futile result. Voltaire, the famous French humanist, boastfully proclaimed, "Fifty years from now the world will hear no more of the Bible." In the year of his boast, the British Museum purchased one manuscript of the Greek New Testament from the Russian government for $500,000 while a first edition of Voltaire's book was selling for eight cents a copy. Fifty years after the death of Voltaire, Bibles were being printed by the Geneva Bible Society in the very house where Voltaire had lived and on his presses.

Thomas Paine, the noted author of the *Age of Reason*, predicted that the Bible would soon be out of print. "When I get through," he announced, "there will not be five Bibles left in America." With the current variety of translations and editions available, many individuals today have more than that number themselves.

The Huguenots portrayed the Bible and Christianity as an anvil surrounded by three blacksmiths. Beneath the picture they inscribed these words:

> The more they pound and the more they shout,
> The more they wear their hammers out!

The indestructibility of God's Word has been verified to this day: "The grass withers, and the flower falls off, but the Word of the Lord abides forever" (1 Peter 1:24-25).

The Influence of the Bible

The Bible claims to be the "living and active" Word of God (Heb. 4:12). It is the instrument God uses to radically transform a life as one is "born again . . . through the living and abiding Word of God" (1 Peter 1:23). As such, it is "the Word of life" (Phil. 2:16). Its message of the Gospel is "the power of God for salvation" (Rom. 1:16). Its truth promises to set men free from bondage (Rom. 8:31-32).

A look at the influence of the Bible throughout history verifies these claims. No other book has had comparable impact for good. The great books of human learning have helped us to understand better the world in which we live, but none has helped to change man himself. Many have pointed out the tragic fact that while our knowledge has literally exploded in the last century in terms of volume, we seem to be less capable than ever before of loving one another and finding peace among men. The endless parade of wars and revolutions is evidence that human learning does not change the heart when it enlarges the mind.

Even the influential writings of other religions have never resulted in lifting and transforming the lives of men and women. For the most part, they present man with rules of life, but the power to effect these rules is absent. In many cases, they only produce a kind of stoic acceptance of present miseries.

The Bible's influence on human societies produces uniquely different results, as seen in the fundamental laws of the highest civilized societies, the social reforms, the raised status of women, the freeing of slaves and in other transformations. Noted men, some of whom were not even believers in the full authority of the Scriptures, have recognized the unique place of the Bible in its influence on man. Immanuel Kant stated, "The existence of the Bible, as a book for people, is the greatest benefit which the human race has ever experienced." Horace Greeley declared, "It is impossible to enslave mentally or socially a Bible-reading people. The principles of the Bible are the groundwork of human freedom." Our contemporary world evidences the truth of Greeley's statement. Where the Bible is genuinely allowed to have an impact and is sincerely believed by peoples, there is the greatest freedom.

The Bible's impact on society at large is best evidenced in its ability to transform individual lives. Augustine, a fifth century Christian leader, struggled for 31 years to find truth and release from a tormenting life in religion and philosophy. One day in a graden in Milan he heard the voice of a neighborhood child chanting, "Take and read! Take and read!" He took up his scroll of the Scriptures and read the first chapter that came to his eyes. When he came to Romans 13:13-14 the Word gripped His life. He shut the book, for a stream of light poured into his soul and all doubt vanished. He became one of the greatest leaders in the church since the Apostles.

Luther, likewise, began the Reformation after God opened his eyes to the truth of a single statement of His Word: "The just shall live by faith" (Hab. 2:4). Countless people from all walks of life have testified and given proof in their lives that the study of, and meditation on, God's Word has a transforming effect that no other writing produces.

The uniqueness of the Bible has been well summed up by Sir Monier-Williams, a professor of Sanskrit who spent 42 years studying the sacred books of the East. He testifies that at first he was impressed by the flashes of truth he found scattered among these writings and that he began to think they shared the message of the Scriptures of Christianity, only to a lesser degree. After further study, however, he completely reversed his thinking, concluding that the main ideas were radically different: they all begin with some flashes of true light, and end in utter darkness. Pile them, if you will, on the left side of your study table; but place your own Holy Bible on the right side—all by itself, all alone—and with a wide gap between them. There is a gulf between it and the so-called books of the East which severs the one from the other utterly, hopelessly, and forever.

4

The Inspiration
of the Bible

The Bible claims to be a book unlike any other. It is the revelation of God to man. Moreover, it supports this claim by displaying certain unusual characteristics which suggest that it is something more than another book penned by human authors. In both content and effect the Bible is unique.

A closer look at the Bible is needed to determine its true nature. Is it the Word of God? Or is it the word of men with special religious insight? Are parts of it the words of God while other parts are the words of men? In seeking answers to these questions, we are involved with what is known as the doctrine of inspiration.

The Meaning of Inspiration

The term "inspiration" applied to the Scriptures comes from the Apostle Paul's statement: "All Scripture is inspired by God" (2 Tim. 3:16). Unfortunately, the meaning of this English word does not clearly reveal the meaning of the Greek word it translates. In fact, it is somewhat misleading. "Inspire" comes from the Latin word *inspiro* which means "to breathe in." Applying this meaning to Scripture would suggest that somehow God breathed into the writings of men, filling them with a certain dynamic quality. This, however, is not what the Apostle is teaching.

The Greek word Paul uses is *theopneustos*. It is a combination of two Greek words, *theos,* "God," and *pneustos,* which is related to the verb meaning "to breathe or blow." The thought in this verb is that of breathing out or expiring and not inspiring or breathing in. *Theopneustos,* therefore, means "breathed out by God." In using this term, the Apostle was not declaring that the Scriptures were breathed into by God but that they are the product of the breath of God. They are in some sense God-breathed writings. From this biblical statement, which refers explicitly to the Scriptures themselves, the term *inspiration* has come to be applied to the entire issue of the nature and extent of divine influence on the human authors so that the whole Bible can also be understood as produced by God.

Some Varying Opinions
Since the time known as the Enlightenment in the 18th century, men have challenged the inspiration of the Scriptures. This period was characterized by the questioning of all traditional authority, including that of the Bible. At its base was the rise of humanistic philosophies which in various ways made man's mind the ultimate source of all meaning. English poet, Alexander Pope, expressed the outcome of these thoughts in his "Essay on Man":

Say first, of God above or man below,
What can we reason but from what we know?
Of man what see we but his station here
From which to reason, or to which refer?
Through worlds unnumbered though the God be known,
Tis ours to trace him only in our own.

The Darwinian theory of naturalistic evolution which arose in the 19th century also had a devastating effect on people's attitudes toward the Bible. By undermining belief in God, the theory of evolution, in the minds of many, reduced the Bible to a purely human book. Even for those who retained some concept of God, evolution weakened the authority of Scripture in that the creation accounts could no longer be taken literally. Certainly, the account of the creation of Adam and Eve could hardly be accepted without considerable reinterpretation.

The theory of evolution was used to explain the development of the religions of man, including that of the Bible. The religion of Israel, some said, evolved from a low stage of polytheism (many gods) and idolatry to henotheism (one God for each nation) and finally to monotheism (one God only) in the time of the prophets of the 8th century B.C. Obviously, some claimed, this required a great deal of restructuring of the Bible. For example, Moses certainly could not have written the first five books with their monotheistic statements (Gen. 1:1), as was traditionally held.

A third important factor, which influenced many people regarding the doctrine of inspiration, was the rise of historical criticism. Drawing on humanistic philosophies and evolution, scholars of the 19th and 20th centuries developed a philosophy of history which held that all things, including the Bible, shared in the flux of history. Everything, supposedly, is conditioned by the historical environment in which it stands. Applied to the Scriptures, this means that a revelation of God for all men and for all times is impossible.

Historical criticism further claimed that the Bible must be approached as any other book. The same questions of historicity should be raised. The method historians use for the evaluation of purported history is known as "the principle of analogy." Only that which is analogous to our human experience and can be explained in terms of human experience can be considered historical.

Such historicism does not necessarily rule out the supernatural; it simply denies that we have any way of verifying its reality. God and His divine interventions in human history remain outside of the realm of history. The tendency of this approach is to explain as many as possible of the miracles of Scripture in terms of natural events. For instance, Jesus walked on a sandbar just below the water's surface instead of miraculously on top. Other events are often interpreted as myths.

Such views naturally triggered widespread discussion of inspiration. Today, it is one of the crucial issues before the church. Not only is it a matter of debate between liberals and evangelical conservatives, but in recent years, the question of the nature of the Bible has become a widely debated issue among evangelicals. Since it directly relates to the question of the authority and certainty of the Christian faith, it is rightfully described as a "watershed" issue of theology. Before turning to the Scriptures themselves, it will be helpful to consider several of the theories of inspiration which have been proposed.

1. *The Bible was written by men who possessed unusual religious insight.* Sometimes this view of inspiration is expressed simply in terms of special natural abilities possessed by gifted artists, poets, or musicians. Others limit it to some believers who are given greater perception of spiritual things than other believers. In neither case, however, is inspiration viewed as a unique work of God.

An illustration of this second view is found in the belief of a recent writer that if great hymnists, like Isaac Watts and Charles Wesley, had lived during the time of David and Solomon "some of their hymns of praise to God would have found their way into the Hebrew canon." Referring specifically to George Matheson's great hymn, "O Love that will not let me go," this writer explains, "this is the kind of inspiration of which the psalms were made. There is no difference in kind. If there is any difference, it is a matter of degree."

Such reasoning fails to note that the greatness of hymns, Christian writings, or sermons by those other than the biblical writers is determined solely by the way they faithfully express biblical truth. In other words, this view confuses the unique work of inspiration and the subsequent ministry of the Spirit in illuminating the inspired writings for believers.

2. *The Bible is only partially inspired.* Different degrees of inspiration are sometimes referred to by this theory. In some portions, God has given only "suggestion" or "direction" to the writers in their use of their ordinary, human knowledge. In other parts there is "direct revelation."

More commonly, however, this position asserts that God inspired the human writers sufficiently to make them infallible in matters of salvation. This is often called infallibility in "matters of faith and practice," or, in other words, in our relationship with God and our walk before Him in the world and in the church. Historical and scientific matters in Scripture were not inspired. They partake of human fallibility, therefore, even as other writings of man. Thus the writers of the Bible, we are told, reveal a prescientific understanding of the universe. They speak of the "pillars" of the earth and of the underworld as if their image of the universe included a flat earth, with heaven above and Hades and the lake of fire beneath. And what was once portrayed as an invasion of evil spirits, we now regard as psychological illness.

This theory of limited inspiration, however, has several problems. First, the Scriptures explicitly declare that "all Scripture is inspired" (2 Tim. 3:16). Nowhere in the Bible is inspiration limited to matters of "faith and practice." Second, no one has been able to show how we can clearly determine the line between matters of faith and nonfaith.

For example, are the stories of the resurrection a matter of history or faith? If there are several historical difficulties in harmonizing the accounts of the four Gospel writers, can we simply say that the record is fallible in its history and yet maintain that somehow the fact of the resurrection comes under the infallible inspiration of God? Such a separation seems impossible. If the historical record is not true, how can we maintain the resurrection as a truth of faith—except on some basis other than the record of Scripture?

One of the values of biblical faith over many ancient religions lies in the fact that it is rooted in history rather than myth. To exclude history from inspiration because of some yet unsolved problems is to weaken this truth. Why should God supernaturally influence the biblical writers in their religious interpretation of His historical saving acts, giving us their meaning infallibly, and at the same time relate their historical setting with fallible human knowledge?

3. *The thoughts of the Bible are inspired, but not the words.* According to this view, God supernaturally inspired the ideas of the biblical writers but they then proceeded to write down the thoughts in their own words. The Scriptures therefore are not verbally inspired.

This theory has at least two grave problems. First, it contradicts the teaching of Scripture on the subject. As we shall see, biblical writers claim over and over that they are declaring the words of God. According to the Apostle Paul, it is the "scripture" or writings which are inspired (2 Tim. 3:16).

Second, from a purely rational point of view it is difficult to conceive of thoughts apart from words. As human beings we think linguistically. In his book *Language and Reality* (Select Bibliographics Reprint, 1939), Wilbur Marshall Urban declares, "It is part of my general thesis that all meaning is ultimately linguistic." Consideration of our own experience shows that this is true. We can convey meaning through gestures, such as a smile, but as soon as we contemplate the meaning of a smile, we find ourselves translating the action into worded concepts. There cannot be an inspiration of thoughts, therefore, which at the same time does not encompass the words through which the thoughts are expressed.

4. The Bible is inspired because it "becomes" the Word of God. Sometimes this view is expressed as "the Bible contains the Word of God." In either case, the Bible is not directly the Word of God. Perhaps no clearer expression of this idea can be found than the following statement of Karl Barth:

> Verbal inspiration does not mean the infallibility of the Biblical word in its linguistic, historical and theological character as human word. It means that the fallible and faulty human word is as such used by God and has to be received and heard in spite of its human fallibility (*Church Dogmatics*, Edinburgh: T. & T. Clark, 1956, I/2, 533).

What the followers of this popular viewpoint believe is that God influenced the writers of the Scripture to be special witnesses of His great acts in the world, especially His revelation in Christ. This influence led them to write about these events and their own encounter with God through these events in such a way that God could use their words to convey His message and to speak to those who read their writings. These writers expressed their thoughts in the language and thought patterns of the day in which they lived.

Frequently, according to some modern scholars, the prophets and apostles used myths such as miracle stories to convey spiritual truth. Much of what appears to be historical reporting must be "demythologized" or stripped of its mythical dress to get at the spiritual truth which is really being conveyed.

Since it is impossible, according to this view, to equate any of the actual statements of the Bible with the Word of God, it is difficult to see how we can really know what God is saying.

Theodore Engelder points out an interesting feature of such thinking when he says that those who advocate this view of the Bible "refuse to believe that God performed the miracle of giving us by inspiration an infallible Bible, but are ready to believe that God daily performs the greater miracle of enabling men to find and see in the fallible word of man the infallible Word of God" (*Christian Dogmatics,* Concordia, 1960). It is obvious that such an interpretation of inspiration, outside of having no support in Scripture, makes the hearing of God's Word a very subjective matter. Different people can hear it differently with no way to decide who is hearing correctly.

5. *The Bible was dictated by God to human authors.* Although this view has been advanced by very few in Christian history, it is commonly supposed to be held by all who believe in the verbal inspiration of the Bible. At least that is the charge. The inspiration of the very words of the Bible means that God must have used the different writers simply as secretaries or transcribers who only wrote down His words as He dictated them.

Leading evangelical writers on the subject, however, have denied this theory repeatedly. When some of the 16th and 17th century Reformers spoke of the Bible as "dictated by the Holy Ghost," they used the term "dictated" only figuratively to express the fact that the human authors wrote the words which God intended. They were in no way intending to deny the reality that the human authors were also actively involved.

Some words, such as the Ten Commandments, which were inscribed directly by God in the stone tablets, did come immediately from God. But when the writings of Scripture as a whole are analyzed, they reveal clearly the different styles and personalities of the individual authors. God in his inspiring work did not set aside the human personalities He created. Rather, He took up the different individuals he had prepared for His service and worked through their own active faculties so that they expressed what He desired. There is a sense in which He uses believers today in a similar way as channels of His work. The only difference is that in the work of inspiration His influence was such that it assured complete truth.

6. *The Bible is completely the inspired Word of God and at the same time the words of the human writers.* The work of in-

spiration involves the activity of the Spirit of God on the human writers so that their words are not only human words but are also the words of God. This position has been the dominant evangelical position throughout the history of the church.

Determining the Doctrine of Inspiration

When we ask ourselves which of the views of inspiration is the correct one, we face again the question of the proper way to seek the answer. Two methods of approach are suggested which almost inevitably lead to opposite conclusions. One proposes that we examine all of the data of the Bible to see if in fact it is completely reliable. Only with such a test can we determine whether it is truly inspired and measure the degree of that inspiration, whether partial or total. The other method proposes to begin with the teaching of the Bible on the subject of inspiration. According to this approach we should carefully interpret all of the scriptural statements that relate to this subject. The summation of this teaching then becomes essentially our doctrine of inspiration.

The difference in the two approaches can be illustrated in the way they deal with certain problems in the Scriptures. Jesus referred to the mustard seed as "smaller than all other seeds" (Matt. 13:32). Botany, however, knows of seeds which are in actuality smaller than the mustard seed. Coming across this biblical statement, which is apparently not strictly true scientifically, the first approach declares that whatever the inspiration of the Bible is, it must be of such a nature that it includes some "errors" such as this one.

The Apostle's statement that "all Scripture is inspired" must be interpreted therefore in some limited fashion so as to allow for this kind of mistake. In other words, this approach affirms that the biblical teaching on inspiration must be interpreted to conform to what we actually find the Scriptures to be by our examination. If we find inaccuracies of history and science, or statements made by one writer which we cannot harmonize with those of other writers we must define inspiration in harmony with these "errors."

The great problem with this approach is that human research and knowledge is made the criterion of truth by which a statement of the Scripture is declared correct or in error. The history of biblical scholarship reveals that these problems have been reduced as new information has been received from areas such as archaeology, and from studies concerning biblical languages and manuscripts. It seems presumptuous to make final judgments on these things today when more information tomorrow may throw new light on them.

The second approach, which seeks to understand the doctrine of inspiration from the direct biblical statements on the subject, must also deal with problems like the mustard seed. But this approach first determines what the Bible teaches about itself, then seeks to harmonize problems such as the mustard seed with that teaching. Assuming for the moment that a careful study of the Scriptures reveals that Christ and the biblical writers teach the full inspiration of all Scripture, this approach seeks an explanation of the problem which is consonant with this teaching. If a problem is found for which there is no adequate solution, it is not considered an adequate basis for changing the explicit teaching of the Scripture. A recognition of the limitation of our present human knowledge must be taken into account.

The way we approach other doctrines of the Bible can help determine which of these two views is correct. The evangelical church has always affirmed the full deity and sinlessness of Christ, based on direct statements, such as John 1:1, that He is God. But suppose we sought to determine whether He was truly God by examining all the statements about Him. Jesus said to the rich young ruler, "Why do you call Me good? No one is good except God alone" (Luke 18:19). Such a statement could easily be interpreted as making Jesus someone less than God, and even making Him a sinner.

On another occasion, Jesus confessed ignorance of the day of His coming again, stating that "the Father alone" knows this information (Mark 13:32). Since one of the attributes of God is omniscience, it would be easy to conclude from this verse that Jesus is not God. But the church did not use such verses to modify the full deity of Christ. Believing scholars gave interpretations of these verses which harmonized with the clear teaching of the deity of Christ and His sinlessness.

The usual method of understanding the teaching of the Scriptures on a given doctrine has always been to start with the explicit statements pertaining to that subject, and this same approach will be used to determine the doctrine of inspiration. In the next chapters the Scriptures will be examined for what they teach concerning their inspiration.

5

The Testimony of the Biblical Writers

When we explore the Scriptures for facts about their own inspiration, some critics object. Such an approach, they say, employs circular reasoning and is therefore unjustified.

We may respond in two ways. First, if we permit a person to speak for himself, and do not off-handedly dismiss his testimony as false, can't we also permit the Bible to speak for itself? Even though he had other witnesses, Jesus testified for Himself. "Even if I bear witness of Myself," He told the Pharisees, "My witness is true" (John 8:14). The truthworthiness of the Bible is attested by external and internal proofs. It deserves to be heeded, therefore, in its claims for itself.

Second, the believing Christian knows that the Bible is the basis of all the great doctrines of the faith, such as the deity of Christ and salvation through His death and resurrection. If we accept the Scriptures as our guide to truth in these areas, shouldn't we also accept their teaching about their own nature?

When we do turn to the Scriptures, we find a veritable avalanche of references speaking to the question of the Bible's character. In this chapter we will look at some of the most important evidence outside of the teaching of Christ. In the next chapter, we will consider Jesus' own view of Scripture, His use of it, and His submission to it.

Two Classic Passages

The consideration of the doctrine of inspiration sends us at once to two key texts—2 Timothy 3:16-17 and 2 Peter 1:20-21. These relate the doctrine of inspiration both to the written Scriptures and to the special influence on the human authors.

1. 2 Timothy 3:16-17. In this passage, the Apostle Paul has just encouraged Timothy, his young son in the faith, to continue in the things he had learned. These included "the sacred writings" which his godly grandmother and mother had taught him from his childhood.

Paul then added an additional thought, perhaps the most important statement in all the Bible concerning inspiration: "All Scripture is inspired by God and profitable for teaching, for reproof, for correction, for training in righteousness; that the man of God may be adequate, equipped for every good work" (2 Tim. 3:16-17).

The opening phrase is translated in the *New English Bible,* "Every inspired Scripture." This may suggest to readers that there are some Scriptures which are not inspired. Most scholars agree, however, that the best rendering of the Greek is "all Scripture is inspired." This is the translation of *The Revised Standard Version* and *The New American Standard Version.* Sometimes the "all" is translated "every" which is also a legitimate rendering of the Greek word, but either way the ultimate meaning is the same. The first wording simply considers the Scripture as a whole, while the second wording views it in its parts.

To understand what the Apostle is saying, we must first determine the meaning of "scripture." The Greek word means simply "a writing" or "that which is written." But among the Jews it came to be used in a special sense for their sacred writings. Paul referred, therefore, to the Old Testament Scriptures which long before His time had been collected into a canon of sacred and authoritative writings.

The New Testament had not yet been completed. There was as yet no final collection of authoritative Christian writings. Legitimate reasons exist, however, for applying Paul's statement to the New Testament as well as to the Old. The term "Scripture" was used by the early church for sacred writings of the New Testament which were received as authoritative alongside the Old Testament.

Suppose we say, "All rain is wet." We do not mean only rain up to that day is moist. Rather, we mean that what we call "rain" is always wet. So the Apostle's statement is a general statement about the nature of Scripture. When the New Testament was added to the sacred writings of the church, it came under this same description.

There is evidence that already in the New Testament time some Christian writings were called "Scriptures." On one occasion Peter compares Paul's writing to "the rest of the Scriptures" implying that Paul's writing was also Scripture (2 Peter 3:16). Clearly, the New Testament writers considered their writings fully on a par with those of the Old Testament. Peter commanded his readers to "remember the words spoken beforehand by the holy prophets and the commandment of the Lord and Saviour spoken by your apostles" (2 Peter 3:2). Paul's statement about inspiration, therefore, may legitimately be applied to our entire Bible.

Looking more closely at the statement itself we find several significant assertions. First, it is the writings which are said to be inspired, not the writers. Obviously, there had to be a work of God upon the writers, but Paul's reference here is to the writings —the words and sentences, if you please.

Second, these writings are declared to be "inspired" which, as we have seen previously, means "God-breathed." We are told, therefore, that the Bible is the product of the breath of God.

The idea of the breath of God was familiar to those acquainted with the Old Testament. It spoke vividly of the creative activity of God through the Holy Spirit. The psalmist declared, "By the word of the Lord the heavens were made, and by the breath of His mouth all their host" (Ps. 33:6). Man himself became a living soul when God "breathed into his nostrils the breath of life" (Gen. 2:7). The same idea appears in Job 33:4: "The Spirit of God has made me, and the breath of the Almighty gives me life." Although the Scriptures had human writers, the Apostle Paul saw beyond them to this ultimate source, the breath of God. It is the creative Holy Spirit, then, who is the final author of the written words of the Bible.

The Apostle said "all" or "every" Scripture is God-breathed, not just some. Nowhere in the Bible is any mention made of a distinction between those parts of the Scripture which relate to faith or salvation and those that pertain to more mundane issues. Objectors to the full inspiration of the Scriptures often note that in verse 15 Paul told Timothy that the sacred writings are able to give "wisdom that leads to salvation." While salvation is certainly the theme of the Bible, it is difficult to see how such a statement permits one to conclude that only the portions of Scripture which speak directly of spiritual truth are inspired. Paul knew nothing of such a division of Scripture. To him, "all Scripture is inspired by God."

2. 2 Peter 1:20-21. If Paul, in 2 Timothy 3:16, informed us of the true nature of Scripture, then the second key passage, by the Apostle Peter, discloses how these supernatural writings were produced. Peter declared, "no prophecy was ever made by an act of human will, but men moved by the Holy Spirit spoke from God" (2 Peter 1:21).

The term *prophecy* in this verse does not refer simply to predictions of the future or even to certain statements made by special individuals called prophets. The word *prophet* means one who speaks the words of God. This meaning is evident from the statements used of Aaron as the spokesman for Moses. When Moses complained of his lack of fluency of speech, God told him to use Aaron, "you are to speak to him and put the words in his mouth . . . he shall speak for you to the people; and it shall come about that he shall be as a mouth for you, and you shall be as God to him" (Ex. 4:15-16). Later, God identified this ministry of Aaron with Moses in these words: "your brother Aaron shall be your prophet" (Ex. 7:1).

In the same way, the prophet of God spoke His words. When God appointed Jeremiah as "a prophet to the nations," Jeremiah showed a lack of confidence in himself and replied to God, "Behold, I do not know how to speak" (Jer. 1:5-6). God's response throws light on the meaning of a "prophet" and the words he spoke: "And all that I command you, you shall speak. . . . Behold, I have put My words in your mouth" (Jer. 1:7-9). Jeremiah later described the true prophet as one who "has stood in the council of the Lord," where he saw and heard God's words and "announced" them to the people (Jer. 23:18, 22).

A prophet was a spokesman for God, so it was natural for the term *prophecy* to refer to any and all of God's Word. It became a common expression in the early church for the entire Old Testament.

The divine influence on the human spokesmen and the writers of Scripture is referred to in Peter's statement that the origin of prophecy was not "an act of human will" but rather came about as "men moved by the Holy Spirit spoke from God." The key word is "moved" or perhaps better "borne along." The Greeks used this same word when a sailing ship was carried along by the wind. When the wind blows the ship moves; when it stops the ship stops. We may also think of a piece of driftwood carried along by a stream of water. Its rate of travel and its direction are totally at the mercy of the water that bears it along.

This word, then, suggests that the writers of Scripture were instruments in the hands of the creative Spirit of God. He directed them when and what to write. This is not to suggest they were like totally passive typewriters. But their activity was under the controlling power of the Holy Spirit. They wrote what He wanted them to write so that in a very real sense He was the author of the writings, as were the humans who penned them.

These two key statements teach us that the written words of Scripture were produced by the breath of God, His creative Spirit. The method of their production was by the controlling influence of the Spirit on the human authors. In both verses, the emphasis falls on the fact that the writings of the Bible are finally not only human words, but the very words God wanted to say.

The Claims to be Writing God's Word

When we consult the biblical writers, we find they claim to have written and spoken God's words. In the first chapter of the Bible, we note the statement, "And God said" repeated at least 10 times. Various other introductory statements permeate the Old Testament Scriptures: "Thus says the Lord" (Amos 1:3); "the Lord spoke to me . . . saying" (Isa. 8:11); "the mouth of the Lord of hosts has spoken" (Micah 4:4). Someone has counted some 3,808 phrases such as these in the Old Testament. Isaiah alone declared at least 20 times that his writings were the "word of the Lord" (see Isa. 1:10). Jeremiah claimed almost 100 times that the word of the Lord came to him (see Jer. 1:2, 4; 2:1). Ezekiel made the same claim some 60 times (see Ezek. 3:16).

The Old Testament writers asserted, further, that they were commanded by God to write His words. Moses said the Lord told him, "Write down these words, for in accordance with these words I have made a covenant with you and with Israel" (Ex. 34:27). Jeremiah related God's similar instructions to him: "Write all the words which I have spoken to you in a book" (Jer. 30:2).

The Holy Spirit was actually speaking through the Old Testament writers; as in the words of Peter, they were "borne along" by Him. Ezekiel declared, "Then the Spirit of the Lord fell upon me, and He said to me, Say, 'thus says the Lord'" (11:5). Among the last words of David are these: "The Spirit of the Lord spoke by me, and His word was on my tongue" (2 Sam. 23:2). In a comprehensive statement summing up God's speaking to His people over the years, Nehemiah said, "Thou didst bear with them for many years, and admonished them by Thy Spirit through Thy prophets" (Neh. 9:30; see also v. 20).

The New Testament writers do not express their claims of inspiration in exactly the same way as those of the Old Testament, especially in their introductory statements. But they make equally high claims for inspiration.

Behind the actual statements of the writers are the promises of Christ to His apostles that they would be taught by the Holy Spirit. In His final discourse with the disciples in the Upper Room, Jesus spoke of the coming of the Holy Spirit who would carry on His ministry among the disciples and even enlarge it. He promised that this coming One would "teach you all things, and bring to your remembrance all that I said to you" (John 14:26).

In addition to remembrance of Jesus' historical teaching, the Spirit would bring new teaching from the Lord after He ascended to heaven. "I have many more things to say to you," Jesus told His disciples, "but you cannot bear them now. But when He, the Spirit of truth, comes, He will guide you into all the truth; for He will not speak on His own initiative, but whatever He hears, He will speak; and He will disclose to you what is to come. He shall glorify Me; for He shall take of Mine and shall disclose it to you" (John 16:12-14).

These verses are often taken as promises of the Spirit's ministry to open the eyes of all believers to the truth of God's Word. This may be a secondary application, but the direct teaching of these statements of Jesus relates to the future ministry of those who were to become His apostles and were commissioned to be His authoritative witnesses (see also John 15:26-27). Their teaching would be His teaching even as He had earlier stated, "the one who listens to you listens to Me" (Luke 10:16; see also Matt. 10:19-20).

The Apostles later made claim to the fulfillment of these promises of their Lord. Paul asserted that he spoke "not in words taught by human wisdom, but in those taught by the Spirit" (1 Cor. 2:13). His Gospel was not received from man but "through a revelation of Jesus Christ" (Gal. 1:12; Eph. 3:3-4, 8). The Thessalonians were absolutely right in receiving his preaching "not as the word of men, but for what it really is, the Word of God" (1 Thes. 2:13) for he had been entrusted with this message by God Himself (Titus 1:2-3).

Peter instructed his readers to "remember the words spoken beforehand by the holy prophets and the commandment of the Lord and Saviour spoken by your apostles" (2 Peter 3:2). In this statement he made two claims. First, he equated his words and those of the other apostles with the words of the Old Testament prophets which, as he had explained, were produced by the influence of the Holy Spirit (1:20-21). Then he affirmed that the apostles spoke "the command of the Lord."

The Apostle John introduced the entire Book of the Revelation as "the Revelation of Jesus Christ, which God gave Him to show to His bondservants" and which was communicated by His angel to His bondservant John (Rev. 1:1). The letters to the seven churches are direct communication from the risen Lord of the church (2:1, 8). Blessing is attached to the acceptance of the words of this revelation. "Blessed is he who reads and those who hear the words of the prophecy, and heed the things which are written in it" (Rev. 1:3). A curse is promised to the one who tampers with any word of it: "I testify to everyone who hears the words of the prophecy of this book: if anyone adds to them, God shall add to him the plagues which are written in this book; and if anyone takes away from the words of the book of this prophecy, God shall take away his part from the tree of life and from the holy city, which are written in this book" (Rev. 22:18-19). Such strong language can only mean that John considered his writing to be the authoritative Word of God.

Many more instances of such claims to revelation could be cited. Never once, however, do we find the Apostles suggesting that only some of what they taught was to be taken as God's Word. In this regard, we should note two statements of Paul which are sometimes misunderstood. In giving instructions concerning the marriage relationship of believer to unbeliever, he uses the words, "I say, not the Lord" (1 Cor. 7:12). By this he does not mean to imply that his words are not the authoritative word of the Lord. A comparison with verse 10 reveals that his reference is to the teaching of Jesus while He was on earth. For a word concerning divorce in general, Paul could call upon the teaching of Jesus (see Matt. 19:3-12). But the issue of a mixed marriage of believer with unbeliever was not discussed by Jesus. Consequently the Apostle could not refer to the Lord's word, but gave his own word as an apostle of Christ.

Another interesting statement of the Apostle appears in the same chapter. Paul concluded his advice for single women in the particular situation at that time with the words, "But in my opinion she is happier if she remains as she is; and I think that I also have the Spirit of God" (1 Cor. 7:40). While this may appear at first glance to be a disclaim to inspiration on the Apostle's part, further study reveals that it is not. While he stated this as his "opinion" and not a direct command of the Lord, he was giving his opinion under the consciousness that "by the mercy of the Lord" he was trustworthy (v. 25) and inspired by "the Spirit of God" (v. 40). He was not simply giving good advice as an ordinary believer.

Scripture as Authorized by God

One of the strongest evidences of the inspiration of the Old Testament is seen in the many citations of these writings in the New Testament. Roger Nicole, professor of theology at Gordon-Conwell Seminary, has counted at least 295 direct references. If we include clear allusions and passages reminiscent of the Old Testament Scripture, the number, according to one scholar, goes up to 4,105.

Not only are these passages cited as absolutely authoritative, but the way in which they are introduced is most significant for our understanding of the biblical teaching of inspiration. This whole area provides a fascinating study, but we must be content with pointing out two ways in which the New Testament writers treat the authorship of the Old Testament. The first is their recognition of the dual authorship, divine and human, of scriptural statements, attested in the following passages: "that what was spoken by the Lord through the prophet" (Matt. 1:22); "David himself said in the Holy Spirit" (Mark 12:36); "the Holy Spirit foretold by the mouth of David" (Acts 1:6); "The Holy Spirit rightly spoke through Isaiah" (Acts 28:35). While we may speak properly of their dual authorship, it is clear from these statements that the biblical writers considered the primary author to be God through His inspiring Spirit.

Our second example is even more direct in showing what the New Testament writers thought about the authorship of the Old Testament. On at least 56 occasions God is said to be the Author. For instance, in Acts 13:34-35, a citation from Isaiah and another from the Psalms are both said to be spoken by God. Of particular interest is the fact that many of the citations are actually the words of men addressed to God in their original Old Testament setting. The Psalms cited in Hebrews 1:7-12 are all spoken by the psalmist in praise to God, yet they are introduced as spoken by God. Similarly, the words of the psalmist, "Today if you hear His voice" (Ps. 95:7), are introduced as the saying of the Holy Spirit (Heb. 3:7). Because He is the speaker, the writer to the Hebrews views these words as presently alive and authoritative even to us who live centuries after the human penman departed.

Aside from the important testimony of our Lord Himself which we will take up in the next chapter, this survey of the way the Bible speaks about its inspiration appears to leave little doubt that the biblical authors believed themselves to be channels of God's special revelation. What they said as His spokesmen they attributed to Him; they claimed to faithfully and truthfully pass this on to their contemporaries and to us. The assertion by William Temple, a recent writer on the subject of the Bible, that, "no single sentence can be quoted as having the authority of a distinct utterance of the All-Holy God," would be totally incomprehensible to the writers of the Scriptures.

6

Christ's View of Scripture

All Christians profess Christ as their Lord. They accept Him as the One who not only has provided salvation, but who directs their lives. Since Christ's direction includes His teaching, Christians have always held His words to be absolutely authoritative. While He was on earth He claimed to speak only the words of His Father who sent Him (John 7:16). The Gospels record that the "multitudes were amazed at His teaching; for He was teaching them as one having authority" (Matt. 7:28-29). His own evaluation of His teaching was, "Heaven and earth will pass away, but My words will not pass away" (Mark 13:31). The words He spoke will judge men at the last day (John 12:48).

All of this is not a plug for a red-letter edition of the Bible, as if the words of Jesus are somehow more authoritative than the rest of Scripture. God, speaking through the prophets and apostles by the Holy Spirit, was the author of all Scripture. Nevertheless, the teachings of Jesus remain particularly important because of who He is—the unique Son of God. If He is our Lord, we must give heed to His teaching concerning the Scriptures, and His attitude toward God's Word must also be ours.

Christ's Acceptance of Scripture
Sometimes we hear that those who walk closely with the Lord and

whose speech and life are saturated with the Bible are "people of the Word." According to the Gospel records, Jesus was the finest example of such a person. One may think that since He was the Son of God and spoke the words of His Father from heaven, He would have little use for the Scriptures. But a glimpse at His life and ministry reveals just the opposite. On every hand we find Him quoting Scripture or alluding to its content in His teaching, and personally submitting His life to its authority.

1. Jesus' frequent use of Scripture. Whether he was struggling with Satan in the temptation, teaching the crowds by the sea, or instructing the disciples, Jesus' words were punctuated with citations from the Old Testament Scriptures. They were on His lips in prayer, even in His suffering on the cross. His mind was so saturated with the words of Scripture that He used them to express His own feelings. The anguish of David centuries earlier became the expression of His own agony as He cried from the cross, "My God, My God, why hast Thou forsaken Me?" (Matt. 27:46) Likewise, His faith was expressed in the words of the psalmist, "Into Thy hand I commit My spirit" (Ps. 31:5, Luke 23:46). Even after His resurrection, we find Him expounding the Scripture.

There are 3,779 verses in the Authorized King James Version of the four Gospels. According to Graham Scroggie, 1,934 of these verses, in whole or in part, contain the words of Christ. Out of these 1,934 verses approximately 180, or close to 1 out of 10 verses of Jesus' recorded teaching, cite or directly allude to the Old Testament.

Moreover, the Lord's references encompass the entire scope of the Old Testament history. Among the many people and events mentioned are the creation of man and the institution of marriage (Matt. 19:4-6), the death of Abel (Matt. 23:35), the days of Noah (Matt. 24:37), the destruction of Sodom (Luke 17:29), Abraham (John 8:56), the appearance of God in the burning bush (Mark 12:26), the life of David (Matt. 12:3), the ministry of Elijah (Luke 4:25), and the martyrdom of the prophet Zechariah (Matt. 23:35). It is interesting to note that in this last reference, Christ spoke of "all the righteous blood shed on earth, from . . . Abel to . . . Zechariah." According to the arrangement of the Old Testament Scriptures in Jesus' time, Genesis stood first and what we know as 2 Chronicles was last. So Jesus encompassed the entire Old Testament canon of Scripture in referring to those who died from Abel to Zechariah.

Similar evidence that He used the entire Scripture is seen in His reference to "the Law of Moses and the Prophets and the Psalms" (Luke 24:44). At that time, the Old Testament was divided into three great parts: the Law, the Prophets, and the Writings. The Psalms were the first part of the Writings. Jesus thus spoke of the entire Old Testament and referred to all of these similarly as "the Scripture" (v. 45). At other times, He referred to the totality of Scripture as "the Law" and "the Prophets" (Matt. 5:17).

2. Jesus' rejection of the views of modern critics. Many modern scholars do not believe that Moses was the author of the first five books of the Bible, often referred to in Scripture as the Law. Yet Jesus frequently referred to the Mosaic authorship of these books. He mentioned Moses as the writer of the Law some 24 times and quoted him 16 times. He stated plainly in John 7:19, "Did not Moses give you the law . . . ?"

It is also popular to ascribe at least two authors and sometimes more to the Book of Isaiah. Chapters 1—39 are said to be written by one person while chapters 40—66 were by a "second" or "deutero" Isaiah. But Jesus quoted from all sections of the book and ascribed the statements to Isaiah. In one particular instance, Jesus cited both from Isaiah 53 and Isaiah 6, ascribing both to the prophet Isaiah (John 12:38-41).

Some of the miraculous events of the Old Testament are also troublesome to many today, especially the happenings of the first chapters of Genesis. Jesus, however, accepted their historicity. According to our Lord, God did create Adam and Eve (Matt. 19:4), Cain and Abel existed (Luke 11:51), and there was a flood in the days of Noah (Matt. 24:38).

Jesus accepted the reality of the destruction of Sodom by fire and brimstone and the story of Lot's wife (Luke 17:29-32). He acknowledged the miracles of Elijah (Luke 4:25-26) and even the much ridiculed record of Jonah and the great fish is attested as reliable by Jesus (Matt. 12:40). We can say, therefore, that no instance appears in Scripture of Jesus questioning the truthfulness of the Old Testament record.

3. Jesus' personal submission to Scripture. Jesus' respect for the Scriptures is not only manifest by the number of times it is found on His lips. It is also seen in the submission of His personal life to its authority. As James said, He was not simply a "hearer" or even a speaker, but a "doer" of the Word (James 1:22-23). Beginning with the temptation of Satan, Jesus resisted the Evil One. The Scriptures gave commands contrary to what Satan was asking and Jesus was determined to obey the Word of God.

Jesus' actions frequently brought charges by the religious leaders that He was breaking the commandments of the Law. But Jesus' reply was always the same. If they understood the true meaning of the laws, they would recognize that He was not violating them in any way (John 7:21 ff). These problems arose, according to Jesus, because the teachers had developed tradition around the Scriptures which actually perverted the Word of God (Matt. 15:6).

His full submission to Scripture is also seen in the way its prophecies compelled Him to walk the road of suffering to death. He described His submission to the vocation which the Father gave Him in terms of the necessity to fulfill Scripture. He must "go to Jerusalem" and be "classed among criminals" because "this which is written must be fulfilled" (Luke 18:31-33; 22:37).

Thus, although He brought new revelation from the Father, Jesus fully accepted the Word of God previously given in the Scriptures. These spoke of Him and were in perfect harmony with His words and life and must be totally fulfilled (Matt. 5:17).

Christ's Use of Scripture

Christ was not only familiar with the Scriptures, having His mind saturated with their truth; He also made continual use of them throughout His ministry. The occasions on which He relied on the Old Testament point to the high value He placed on its absolute authority in all matters.

1. The basis of His teaching. Despite the fact that Jesus received revelation from the Father, much of His teaching was based on the words of Old Testament Scripture. Included were fundamental themes as well as teachings of a more incidental nature. His proclamation of the kingdom was derived from the prophecies, especially Daniel (Matt. 4:17; Dan. 2:44). In His conversation with Nicodemus, Jesus hinted that the truth of the new birth should have been known to a ruler in Israel because Ezekiel and others had spoken about it (John 3:5; Ezek. 36:25-27).

In response to the question on divorce, Jesus based His theology of marriage on the Genesis account of Creation. God had made man male and female and the two became one flesh. This was the teaching of Scripture and, thus, the will of God (Matt. 19:4-6). On another occasion, Jesus summed up His understanding of man's ultimate duty before God, in the words of Deuteronomy 6:5: "You shall love the Lord your God with all your heart, and with all your soul, and with all your mind" (Matt. 22:37). Even the so-called golden rule of ethics, "whatever you want others to do for you, do so for them," was in reality, He said, the essence of "the Law and Prophets."

The words spoken by the prophet Isaiah centuries earlier to the people of his day applied also to the scribes and Pharisees of the first century: "This people honors Me with their lips, but their heart is far away from Me. But in vain do they worship Me, teaching as their doctrines the precepts of men" (Matt. 15:8-9; citing Isa. 29:13).

Sometimes it was only a brief phrase or thought that was applicable to a given situation. Jesus found the descriptive phrase "sheep without a shepherd," which was used several times in the Old Testament, a very appropriate description of the multitudes in His own day (Matt. 9:36; Num. 27:17; Ezek. 34:5). Again, He warned against grabbing the place of honor lest someone be present who deserves it more (Luke 14:7-11), a truth already found in Proverbs 25:6-7. His statement about the continual presence of the poor was based on a direct statement to that effect in Deuteronomy 15:11.

Many other instances could be cited, but these are sufficient to demonstrate that Jesus found the Old Testament a rich source for His own teaching. Even more significant is His claim that He spoke not on His own, but the words He had been taught by the Father (John 8:28; 12:50). The Old Testament may be seen, therefore, as the Father's own instruction.

Above all, Jesus used the Scriptures to interpret His own Person and mission in the world. We have already noted how, after the Resurrection, He used the entire Old Testament canon to instruct His disciples on the things concerning Himself. But long before this He had referred to the fulfillment of Scripture in Himself. He had come, He said, "not . . . to abolish, but to fulfill" the Law and the prophets (Matt. 5:17). The ministry of John the Baptist, which pointed to Him, was in fulfillment of Isaiah's prophecy that a messenger would be sent to prepare the way before the Lord (Matt. 11:10). And Jesus inaugurated His ministry at Nazareth by taking up the scroll in the synagogue and reading from Isaiah 61:1, "The Spirit of the Lord is upon Me, because He anointed Me to preach the Gospel to the poor" (Luke 4:18). He then declared these words to be fulfilled in Himself (v. 21).

On one occasion, when the disciples of John questioned whether He really was the "Coming One," Jesus validated His identity by pointing to His miracles, which fulfilled the prophecy Isaiah had given for the Messiah and His times (Matt. 11:1-6; see Isa. 35:5-6).

Nowhere is Jesus' interpretation of His action as the fulfillment of Scripture more evident than in the work at Calvary. He walked this road in submission to the purpose of God as told in the Scriptures. In His obedience He was also declaring Himself to be the fulfillment of the Scriptures. This is highlighted in His words toward the end of His agony on the cross. Having previously noted that His betrayal, arrest, separation from the disciples, and death were all in fulfillment of Scripture, Jesus came to the very end and was still concerned with the prophecies that were being fulfilled in Him. John's Gospel records that "Jesus, knowing that all things had already been accomplished, in order that the Scripture might be fulfilled, said, 'I am thirsty' " (19:28).

Even the rather incidental statement of the Psalmist about the distasteful drink which God's suffering servant would receive from His persecutors had to be fulfilled in Him (see Ps. 69:21). When Jesus had drunk, "He said, 'It is finished!' And He bowed His head and gave up His spirit." When everything the Scripture had predicted of Him was complete, He had accomplished the appointed course of suffering the Father had given Him for our salvation.

2. *The final appeal in debate.* The teaching of Jesus cut across

much of the religious thinking of His day, and He was frequently challenged by those who heard Him. On some occasions, He sought to open their eyes to truth through probing questions of His own. In these confrontations with opponents, Jesus always appealed to Scripture as His final authority.

In the parable of the vineyard, Jesus told a story which clearly pricked the consciences of His hearers, who were rejecting Him as the Son of God (Luke 20:16-17). In the story, the result of the rejection was the transfer of the vineyard from the unbelieving Jews to others who would receive God's true messenger. Those listening refuted His words with the cry, "May it never be!" (v. 16) Jesus countered their retort with an appeal to Scripture: "What then is this that is written, 'The stone which the builders rejected, this became the chief cornerstone'?" (v. 17) For Jesus, this Scripture applied to His present situation, and because Scripture was absolutely authoritative, their objection was overruled.

His antagonists frequently sought to entrap Him with subtle questions. On one occasion, the Sadducees, who did not believe in the resurrection, thought they had disproven the resurrection with the question about the hypothetical woman who had married seven brothers successively in this life (Matt. 22:23-33). They wanted to know whose wife she would be in the resurrection.

Jesus countered with the statement, "You are mistaken, not understanding the Scriptures, or the power of God" (v. 29), and proceeded to give them a brief lesson in the proper understanding of Scripture: "Regarding the resurrection of the dead, have you not read that which was spoken to you by God, saying, 'I am the God of Abraham, and the God of Isaac, and the God of Jacob'? God is not the God of the dead but of the living" (vv. 31-32).

His argument hinged on the little word "am." Abraham, Isaac, and Jacob had passed from the earth, but God was still their God, proving there was life after death and a resurrection. It is interesting to note that, according to Jesus, God spoke in words that could be "read."

On another occasion, when the Pharisees challenged Jesus about the action of His disciples on the Sabbath, Jesus responded with the words, "have you not read in the Law . . . ?" (Matt. 12:5) Their error was not only in ignoring the Scripture, but in failing to understand its true meaning. So the Lord instructed them, "But if you had known what this means, 'I desire compassion, and not a sacrifice,' you would not have condemned the innocent" (v. 7; citing Hosea 6:6).

Again and again in debates with opponents, Jesus cited Scripture as His final court of appeal. Even in the serious charge of blasphemy, His answer was, "Has it not been written . . . ?" (John 10:34) The right use of Scripture could not be refuted, nor did Christ ever question which portions were authoritative. If the Scriptures said it, that was enough.

Christ's Explicit Teaching on Scripture

Christ placed absolute confidence in the Scriptures for His own Person and for His ministry with others. All of this implies a belief in the final authority of Scripture. No one would place such trust in writings unless he believed they were the words of God Himself.

It is true that we do not find long discourses by Jesus on the nature of the Bible. His contemporaries never once questioned His reliance on Scripture, for they too had a high view of the Scriptures, believing them to be sacred writings. Interspersed in the teaching of Jesus, however, are several explicit statements about Scripture, which give us His understanding of their nature. Here are some of the most important.

1. Matthew 5:17-18. Because Jesus rejected the legalistic religion of many of His contemporaries, He was charged with disregarding the Old Testament Scriptures and violating the commandments. He replied with words that make His viewpoint of these writings absolutely clear, "Do not think that I came to abolish the Law or the Prophets; I did not come to abolish, but to fulfill. For truly I say to you, until heaven and earth pass away, not the smallest letter or stroke shall pass away from the Law, until all is accomplished."

By "Law" and "Prophets" Jesus was using terms which meant the entire Old Testament writings. These writings, He said, looked forward to the fulfillment of God's plan. Everything they said was absolutely true and would be completely accomplished. To emphasize His point, Jesus referred to the smallest letter in the Hebrew alphabet, smaller than our English "i", and to a tiny stroke which distinguishes one Hebrew letter from another, smaller but comparable to the stroke which differentiates E from F. Our English equivalent might be not one "t" will be uncrossed or an "i" undotted.

So in these words, Jesus declared the absolute authority of the Scriptures down to the very detail. Some of these Scriptures, such as those that ordered the sacrifices, were to find their accomplishment in Christ and be superceded, but as God's Word they stood as true and had to be fulfilled.

2. *John 10:34-36.* One of the classic statements regarding the nature of Scripture is found in Christ's defense of His claim to be God. In answer to the charge of blasphemy, Jesus made an interesting appeal to Scripture: "Has it not been written in your law, 'I said, you are gods'? If He called them gods, to whom the Word of God came (and the Scripture cannot be broken), do you say of Him, whom the Father sanctified and sent into the world, 'You are blaspheming', because I said, 'I am the Son of God'?"

Jesus' reasoning was, "If the Scriptures call the human judges of Israel 'gods' without blasphemy, then how can you charge me with blasphemy because I claim to be the Son of God?" While Jesus certainly claimed to be the Son of God in a far higher sense than the judges of old, He used this approach to repel the immediate charge of blasphemy so He could get His opponents to consider more fully His right to this claim (vv. 37-38).

The point for our discussion, however, is found in His statement, "the Scripture cannot be broken." The citation about "gods" comes from Psalm 82:6 which Jesus interestingly calls "Law" (v. 34), showing that He considered not only the commandments as authoritative, but all of the Old Testament. He described these synonymously as "Scripture," and declared they cannot be broken. The word "broken" was commonly used in the sense of causing the commandments to lose their force and, consequently, rendering them no longer binding.

Jesus taught that Scripture possesses a character impossible to be voided or anulled, and its flawless authority belongs to each word.

3. *Matthew 19:4 ff.* One final passage, though not directly speaking of the nature of the Scriptures, explains Jesus' concept of them. In His discussion of marriage, He cited Genesis 2:24. When we read this text in Genesis it appears as a statement of

Moses, the human author, and not as a direct word from God. Jesus, however, took these words as spoken by God when He introduced them: "Have you not read, that He who created them from the beginning made them male and female and said . . . ?" It is not only the statements introduced by a formula such as, "Thus says the Lord," that constitute the words of God. Everything in Scripture is spoken by Him, as well as by the human writer involved.

Our Attitude Toward Christ's Teaching

Jesus held a high view of the Scriptures. For Him, they were the inspired words of God. Many liberal critics of Scripture, who put the Bible on a much lower plane, acknowledge that Jesus believed in an inerrant Bible.

Several explanations have been proposed seeking to account for Jesus' words while at the same time rejecting them as valid for us. Some believe that He was simply accommodating Himself to the belief of His contemporaries. He appealed to the authority of the Old Testament because his audience believed it was inspired, not because He did. Such an explanation fails on at least two counts. First, the Gospel records make it clear that Jesus did not hesitate to challenge His contemporaries when He disagreed with them. Why should He accommodate their alleged error in the case of the Scriptures? Second, it is impossible to believe that He could repeatedly relate Himself and His ministry as the fulfillment of the Old Testament and at the same time believe they were only human writings filled with fallacies.

Others seek to account for the teachings of Jesus by declaring that when He became a man His knowledge was limited. This limitation included the possibility of mistaken ideas. Much could be said in reply to this suggestion but again two comments must suffice. First, limitation does not necessarily involve error. But more importantly, Jesus claimed to speak the truth. If He was mistaken about the Scripture on which He grounded His teaching, it is difficult to see why He should be trusted elsewhere.

There is no way round the implication of these clear teachings of Christ for the believer. The testimony of H.C.G. Moule concerning this issue should be weighed seriously by every Christian. Referring to Christ, Bishop Moule declared, "He absolutely trusted the Bible; and though there are in it things inexplicable and intricate that have puzzled me so much, I am going, not in a blind sense, but reverently, to trust the Book because of *Him*" (John Battersby Harford and Frederick Charles MacDonald, *The Life of Bishop Moule*. London: Hodder and Stoughton, 1922, p. 138).

7

Inspiration
and Inerrancy

Are all parts of the Bible equally inspired? Does inspiration extend to the very words of Scripture? Does the biblical teaching of inspiration mean that the Bible is inerrant? These questions are fraught with misconceptions and have become centers of controversy. A brief survey of the history of the doctrine of inspiration since the time of the New Testament will help determine what position was commonly taught in the church.

Verbal-Plenary Inspiration
Jesus and the biblical writers held a high view (known as a verbal-plenary concept) of the inspiration of the Scriptures. A variety of definitions have been given for this position. Charles Hodge, in *Systematic Theology,* defines inspiration as "an influence of the Holy Spirit on the minds of certain select men, which rendered them the organs of God for the infallible communication of His mind and will."

Benjamin B. Warfield, perhaps the greatest defender of this position on inspiration in the last century, described inspiration as "a supernatural influence exerted on the sacred writers by the Spirit of God, by virtue of which their writings are given Divine trustworthiness."

The control of the Spirit in the inspiration of the Scriptures assured their infallibility. Certain men were supernaturally influenced by the Holy Spirit and wrote God's Word without error in the original manuscripts. Two important truths are included in this concept: (1) the extent of inspiration and (2) the process.

1. The extent of inspiration. The extent of inspiration is entailed in the words *plenary* and *verbal.* By *plenary,* we mean that all of Scripture is inspired—its God-breathed quality is absent from no parts, however mundane they may seem. This is not to say that all Scripture is on the same level of importance. Certain portions of Chronicles, for instance, are not as central to the Christian faith as the Book of Romans. But they are no less inspired.

On this point, we may compare the Scriptures to our own bodies. Certain parts may not be as significant as our hearts, but they are no less living parts of our bodies. In the same way, different parts of Scripture perform different functions, some more humble than others, but all form an organic whole.

Plenary inspiration means that all of Scripture partakes of the same degree of inspiration. Some of the content came by direct revelation from God, while in other portions, such as the genealogical records, the writers obviously had access to historical documents. But this difference in revelational level does not imply a difference in inspiration. Inspiration applies to the written word. It is the Scriptures, the sacred writings, that Paul declared were God-breathed (2 Tim. 3:16).

Such a plenary concept of inspiration is evident in the attitude of Christ and the biblical writers. They did not distinguish between inspired, more inspired, and uninspired portions of Scripture. All Scripture was recognized as belonging to a whole that carried absolute divine authority.

To deny the plenary inspiration of the Bible requires a judge to determine what is and what is not inspired. Such an action is foreign to biblical teaching and practice, and would leave the church with a Bible of limited authority. The final authority rests with the critics who presume to ferret out the inspired portions. J. C. Ryle, nineteenth century writer and Bishop of Liverpool, pointed out the dangerous result of assuming anything less than full inspiration:

We corrupt the Word of God most dangerously, when we throw any doubt on the plenary inspiration of any part of Holy Scripture. This is not merely corrupting the cup, but the whole fountain. This is not merely corrupting the bucket of living water, which we profess to be present to our people, but poisoning the whole well. Once wrong on this point, the whole substance of our religion is in danger. It is a flaw in the foundation. It is a worm at the root of our theology. Once allow the worm to gnaw the root, and we must not be surprised if the branches, the leaves, and the fruit, little by little, decay. The whole subject of inspiration, I am aware, is surrounded with difficulty. All I would say is, notwithstanding some difficulties which we may not be able to solve, the only safe and tenable ground to maintain is this—that every chapter, and every verse, and every word in the Bible has been given by inspiration of God. We should never desert a great principle in theology any more than in science, because of apparent difficulties which we are not able at present to remove.

To say the inspiration of Scripture is *verbal* means that inspiration extends to the very words of Scripture. The prophets were those in whose mouths God placed His words (see Jer. 1:9). The Apostle Paul spoke in words taught by the Spirit (1 Cor. 2:13). The words of Scripture are considered to be the words of God (see Matt. 19:4-5). On several occasions, the arguments of Christ and the biblical writers rested on specific words. The use of the word "gods" by the psalmist was the key to Jesus' rebuttal of the Jews' charge of blasphemy (John 10:34-35). The fact that the promise of God recorded in Genesis said "seed" rather than "seeds" was significant for the Apostle Paul's argument to the Galatians (Gal. 3:16).

Aside from this biblical evidence, which seems conclusive, there is really no other way in which one can think of the inspiration of the Scriptures except that inspiration extends to each word. To speak of the inspiration of the thoughts, but not the words, is impossible. Thoughts take shape and are expressed in words. The meaning and accuracy of an expression is directly related to the words used. It is often implied that focusing on the words of Scripture means you miss the spiritual vitality of the thoughts. But as Eric Sauer points out, the spirit involved in the thought is conveyed through the word. "The word may be regarded as the body of the thought, giving the spirit 'visibility' and form; therefore if the word is blurred the thought is blurred and all becomes foggy and indistinct. The saying 'spirit without word' is therefore a 'word without spirit,' that is, a spiritless (meaningless) word."

There was no question in Jesus' mind but that meaningful thoughts are conveyed through words. Speaking of His "words," He said they "are spirit and are life" (John 6:63). Charles Spurgeon summed up the matter well when he said, "We contend for every word of the Bible and believe in the verbal, literal inspiration of Holy Scripture. Indeed, we believe there can be no other kind of inspiration. If the words are taken from us, the exact meaning is of itself lost."

When we speak of the very words of the Bible as "inspired" we must hasten to add that we are referring specifically to the words of the original manuscripts or writings. None of the original writings are known to have survived and are therefore not available to us today. Our Bibles are based on copies of the originals. The great number of copies and the care the copyists took (which is known from historical records) enabled scholars through the science of textual criticism to come very close to duplicating the original texts. There are certain minor variations for which we still cannot be absolutely sure of the exact words of the original text. If we want to speak technically, therefore, we must say that our present Bibles partake of verbal inspiration in so far as they reproduce accurately the message expressed in the words which were first written by God's chosen human instruments.

2. *The process of inspiration*. The exact nature of the process of inspiration remains a mystery even as do the manifold works of God within man. How God brings about the new birth and then proceeds to work in a human heart to shape a believer into the image of His Son is not fully known. Certainly, we are not always conscious of such activity within ourselves. We believe that God is at work in us accomplishing His will even as we are actively involved ourselves. The Apostle Paul spoke of the relation of human and divine activity when he exhorted the Philippian believers to "work out your salvation . . . for it is God who is at work in you" (Phil. 2:12-13).

The biblical doctrine of inspiration teaches that God, by His Spirit, worked through the biblical writers in such a way that their own individual personalities were actively involved in the expression of the message. For some, the divine impetus came on them strongly like a fire (Jeremiah) or the roaring of the lion (Amos), while others evidenced no such consciousness of divine power. Despite the variety of psychological experience among the writers, the end product was equally inspired.

Evidence of the different human personalities is easily recognized. The poetic style of the psalmists stands in contrast to the analytical and logical structure of the Apostle Paul's writings. A short reading of the writings of the Apostle John and of Luke will reveal a vast difference in vocabulary and literary style. Jeremiah is often called the "weeping prophet" because of the mournful and melancholic strains that are felt in his writings.

In addition to differences in style and vocabulary, the personalities of the biblical writers were often directly involved in their messages as they wrote of firsthand experiences. Isaiah's vision of "the Lord sitting on a throne, lofty and exalted" was directly related to his own call to the ministry (Isa. 6). The psalmist expressed his experience when he wrote, "I have been young, and now I am old; yet I have not seen the righteous forsaken, or his descendants begging bread" (Ps. 37:25). The very culture in which the writers lived shows through their writings. Paul's numerous references and illustrations from Greco-Roman life—military, athletic, and legal—reflect his personal historical setting.

All these human elements show the Bible is truly a human book as well as divine. How the Spirit could use human instruments to produce the message He desired is not totally understandable to us. But there is an interesting analogy to the production of Scriptures in the coming of the Son of God to earth. The Holy Spirit came upon Mary, who was truly human and fallible. Yet through her, by means of a normal development following supernatural conception, the Son of God became human flesh and was born truly man. He bore fully the characteristics of a man as well as of God. *[margin note: Christ as an example of inspiration]*

Even as the sinful element in Mary was overruled so as not to contaminate the Lord, so the sinful fallibility of the human authors was overruled and what was produced was without flaw.

The Spirit of God came on human sinful writers and so worked in them to produce divine-human writings. The exact process remains mysterious.

Inerrant Inspiration

Does verbal-plenary inspiration mean inerrant inspiration? That is, do the biblical teachings on inspiration result in an inerrant Word of God, the Bible? This question is important and deserves close attention.

1. The meaning of inerrancy. The issue of inerrancy is often confused by the terminology used. Some would acknowledge the infallibility of the Bible but deny its inerrancy. Others do not like the word inerrancy because it is a negative term. It will be best at the outset to clarify what we mean by these terms.

The dictionary gives the first meaning of infallibility as, "not fallible; not liable to err." The same source defines inerrancy as, "exempt from error; free from mistake; infallible." Unless we give our own meanings to these words, in ordinary usage *infallibility* and *inerrancy* are essentially synonymous terms. Where these terms are distinguished in discussing the Bible, infallibility is generally applied to the fundamental message of the Scriptures concerning salvation and man's relationship to God. *Inerrancy,* on the other hand, is related to all the contents of Scripture. Used this way, many would advocate an infallible Bible but not one that is inerrant. Care must be taken to understand exactly what a speaker or writer means when he uses these words.

Because of confusion over the term *infallibility,* we will use the term *inerrancy.* Applied to the Scriptures, *inerrancy* means, simply, that the Bible is without error; it does not contain mistakes. All its statements accord with truth.

2. What the Bible teaches about inerrancy. Although the Bible does not use the word inerrant, its doctrine of inspiration and the statements which describe the nature of the contents of the Bible appear to lead to the conclusion of inerrancy. We have seen that Christ and the biblical writers believed that the totality of the Scripture is the inspired Word of God. Paul's declaration that "all Scripture is inspired" (2 Tim. 3:16), and the words of our Lord that "Scripture cannot be broken" (John 10:35) are comprehensive. Moreover, we have seen how they referred to specific words of Scripture as absolutely authoritative. Never is a suggestion made that a part of Scripture is untrustworthy or in some way uninspired.

Certain statements describing the Scriptures also support the absolute inerrancy of the Bible. The Psalmist declared, "the sum of Thy word is truth" (Ps. 119:160); "All His precepts are sure" (Ps. 111:7), "the law of the Lord is perfect . . . the testimony of the Lord is sure . . . the judgments of the Lord are true . . ." (Ps. 19:7-9). The writer of Proverbs similarly stated, "Every word of God is tested" (Prov. 30:5). Individual writers claim absolute truthfulness. Luke stated the purpose of his writing, that "you might know the exact truth" (Luke 1:4). The Greek word for truth is related to the negative of a word meaning "to trip up," the thought being a reliability in which there is no tripping up. John also testified he was "telling the truth" (John 19:35).

When we place these statements alongside the total teaching on the inspiration and authority of the Bible it seems impossible not to conclude that the Bible teaches its inerrancy. Such teaching is absolutely compatible with the claims of the biblical writers to be speaking and writing God's Word. He is preeminently "the God of Truth" (Isa. 65:16) who never lies (Titus 1:2). To affirm errors in the Bible is to make it difficult to trust the Scriptures as the revelation of God's truth.

It is necessary, when speaking of the truthfulness of a statement, to explain further what is meant. For instance, we may truthfully record a statement which is in itself a lie. We may speak generally of something in round numbers that are not exactly true on the level of scientific accuracy. What the writer intended in his statement is therefore all important. Applying this to biblical inerrancy, we mean that the Bible is without error when the Scriptures are understood according to the intention of the writers.

Several questions need to be asked when we approach the statements of Scripture. First, is the author portraying the statement as true or simply reporting a lie? In Genesis, Moses recorded the lie of Satan when he said to the woman, concerning the eating of the forbidden fruit, "You surely shall not die!" (Gen. 3:4) Inerrancy here is the truthfulness and accuracy of this report.

Second, we must ask, does the author intend to speak in

popular, phenomenal language or in technical scientific language? We speak of the sun rising and setting, which is true from our perspective. But scientifically, the earth moves, not the sun. We do not charge our newspapers with error when they give us the time for the sunrise and sunset.

Third, the author may speak in round numbers rather than intending exactness. If the number is a reasonable approximation there is no untruth involved.

Finally, we must seek to determine whether the author is intending to speak literally or through a figure of speech. Some would charge the biblical writers with belief in an erroneous cosmology in speaking of "the four corners of the earth" (Isa. 11:12) or the "windows of heaven" (Gen. 7:11, KJV). When such language is understood in a figurative sense, as it was undoubtedly intended, no error is involved.

Sometimes, the issue of grammatical error is raised when a construction is found that does not follow the usual patterns. Whether we speak and write with good grammar has nothing to do with the truthfulness of a statement. Moreover, good reasons can usually be found for those instances in which the biblical writers vary from normal grammatical expression.

Inerrancy, therefore, means that when full consideration is given to the statements of Scripture in light of their intended meaning and use by the author, the Bible is fully trustworthy in all it states. Its primary teaching is related to God's great redemptive program through Christ. But in the accomplishment of this salvation God invaded our world to deal with us in our history and geography, and so the record of God's salvation touches other areas of knowledge as well as spiritual truth. It is this record, in its entirety, that is the inspired, inerrant word of God. This does not mean the writers knew more about history and science than our modern experts, or that they were omniscient in all fields. It means they were preserved from misleading us in any statement, no matter how insignificant.

Inerrancy in Church History

The belief of the church cannot be our final source of authority. That must always be the Scriptures. It is interesting, nevertheless, to note what the leaders of the church have taught on this subject. In the second century Justin Martyr, a church father, said, "We must not suppose that the language proceeds from the men who are inspired, but from the Divine Word which moves them." About the same time, Irenaeus, Bishop of Lyons, declared, "All Scripture, as it has been given to us by God, will be found to be harmonious." One of the greatest men in church history, Augustine, spoke of "the revered pen of the Spirit" in regard to the Scripture, and testified in a letter to Jerome, "I have learned to defer this respect and honor to those Scriptural books only which are now called canonical, that I believe most firmly that no one of these authors has erred in any respect in writing." Martin Luther asserted, "The entire Scriptures are assigned to the Holy Ghost," and, "the Scriptures cannot err." Calvin repeatedly affirmed his belief in the inspiration of the Scriptures, and on one occasion said that "we . . . feel perfectly assured—as much so as if we beheld the divine image visibly impressed in it [Scripture]—that it came to us, by the instrumentality of men, from the very mouth of God."

Such statements could be multiplied over and over from the church leaders up to the eighteenth century when the critical view began to attack the authority of Scripture. The statement of the respected scholar Kirsop Lake, written in 1926, well sums up the tradition of the church on this subject. Clearly in opposition to a high view of inspiration, he nevertheless wrote:

It is a mistake often made by educated persons who happen to have but little knowledge of historical theology, to suppose that fundamentalism is a new and strange form of thought. It is nothing of the kind; it is the partial and uneducated survival of a theology which was once universally held by all Christians. How many were there, for instance, in Christain churches in the eighteenth century who doubted the infallible inspiration of all Scripture? A few, perhaps, but very few. No, the fundamentalist may be wrong; I think that he is. But it is we who have departed from the tradition, not he, and I am sorry for the fate of anyone who tries to argue with a fundamentalist on the basis of authority. The Bible and the *corpus theologicum* of the Church are on the fundamentalist side (Kirsop Lake, *The Religion of Yesterday and Tomorrow*. Boston: Houghton, 1926, p. 61).

8

Dealing with Problems in the Bible

A careful student of the Bible will come across problems in the pages of Scripture which seem incompatible with their full inspiration. Skeptics and critics use these problems to undermine the reliability of the Bible. Bible-believing scholars, however, have always recognized these problems and have sought to resolve them in agreement with the biblical teaching of inspiration.[1]

The Cause of Problems

We might assume, in light of the doctrine of inspiration, that no difficulties would be encountered in Scripture. Everything should check out and harmonize perfectly. A little thought on the nature of the Bible, however, quickly dispels this idea.

When we consider the age and variety of cultures encountered in Scripture, it should not surprise us that there are things we presently do not understand. Our current culture is not like that of our forefathers and certain practices or idioms pertaining to their way of life may not be known to us. Archeological and historical research has aided immensely in clearing up problems.

One interesting example that illustrates the nature of these difficulties is the chronological records for the time of Israel's kings. At least two different calendars were used for long periods of history, one year beginning in the spring and another beginning in the fall. We, of course, do something similar when we employ fiscal and civil calendars which do not coincide.

In addition, the Hebrew Chroniclers used two different systems in computing the years of a king's reign. According to one system, any part of a calendar year was considered to be one year's reign. Thus, for example, using our calendar, if a king assumed the throne in December of one year, he completed his first year at the end of December and began his second on January 1. According to the other system the first year of rule commenced with January no matter what portion of the previous year the king had already reigned. It is obvious that without the knowledge of these systems, many chronological problems would be impossible to solve. As archeologists and historians continue to find new data such problems are diminishing.

Some difficulties in Scripture relate to the fact that we do not possess the original copies. The Scriptures we possess are based on manuscripts that were copied over and over by hand. As careful as the copyists attempted to be, inadvertent mistakes inevitably crept in.

An obvious instance is found in the numbers of 2 Kings 24:8 and 2 Chronicles 36:9. According to the Kings account, Jehoiachin became King when he was 18 years old and reigned 3 months before he was taken captive. Chronicles, however, states that he was only 8 years old when he began reigning, but he reigned 3 months and 10 days. This is obviously a contradiction caused by a copyist error. Since 18 is written in Hebrew as "eight" and "ten," it seems clear that the "ten" was misplaced. It was correctly joined to the eight in Kings—making 18—but was omitted in Chronicles and picked up later as 10 days. In fact, some of the manuscripts of the Greek and Syriac translations of Chronicles have Jehoiachin 18, as in Kings. Such copying mistakes do not account for a large number of discrepancies, but they are present and should alert us to consider this possibility for error.

Certain problems should be expected when we think of the true nature of the Bible. The Spirit of God worked through real people to produce Scripture. He did not obliterate their personalities or lift them out of their historical situations to place them on some kind of special plane where they all thought and expressed themselves alike. They each brought the Word of God into their own situations with different needs and with unique expressions. It should not be surprising if everything does not immediately appear in perfect agreement. In fact, such agreement might be taken as evidence against the authenticity of the Scriptures, suggesting that there was collaboration and forgery on the part of whoever wrote it.

Thus, the presence of problems does not overturn the doctrine of inspiration. Throughout the history of the church, believers have held to the inspiration of the Scriptures, while fully aware of these problems. They have searched for solutions and have answered many of the problems, as we will see. But their inability to answer every one was never considered sufficient cause to abandon what they believed the Bible taught about itself.

Doctrinal and Moral Problems

Certain questions surface when we consider some of the doctrinal and ethical statements of the Bible. In most instances these are readily solved when we fully understand what the Bible actually says. In other instances, however, the difficulty arises when a critic of Scripture simply does not agree with the ethics of the Bible. We can label these as problems with inspiration only if we assume that the objector's view is infallible.

The instigation of David's numbering of the people is often cited as a theological contradiction. In 2 Samuel 24:1 we read that God incited David to number Israel and Judah. However, in 1 Chronicles, Satan is said to have "moved David to number Israel" (21:1). Some say that this is indicative of two theologies, one in which God controls the world and the other in which Satan is in control. The solution is not difficult when we understand something about the relationship between God and Satan. God often allows Satan to perform his evil deeds for some greater purpose. Thus God, in this instance, is presented as the ultimate Cause for Satan moving David to this act. Parallel situations are found in God permitting Satan to attack Job (Job 1:12; 2:6) and in His sending an evil spirit to trouble Saul (1 Sam. 16:14).

In seeking solutions to problems such as these, it is important that we have a full understanding of the biblical teaching about a given subject. One verse often brings out one side of the issue and another looks at it from a different side. While the two sides seem contradictory, in reality they are parts of the whole truth.

In addition, we must take care to understand words in their own contexts. The alleged difficulty between Paul and James over justification is easily solved when we consider the particular way they used similar words. Paul declared that we are justified by faith without works (Rom. 4:5; Eph. 2:8-9). But James declared that justification comes by faith and works (James 2:24). If we examine the use of the words "faith" and "works," however, we find that James and Paul do not mean exactly the same thing by these words.

By "faith" James meant that kind of mental assent that even the demons possess (James 2:19). Such faith or belief, he said, is not sufficient to save. It must be a faith instead that is living and gives evidence of life in works. Works to him were the outworking of saving faith.

Paul, on the other hand, meant by "faith" a genuine belief that issues in action. He spoke of a faith that works through love (Gal. 5:6). When he opposed "works" and "faith," he meant works of a legal nature by which people supposed that they could gain merit before God.

Thus, when we consider the meaning of the words in their contexts, both Paul and James believed the same thing. Each was only emphasizing a certain facet of the truth. Paul believed that we are saved only by faith, but a faith that is alive and working. James likewise believed that we are saved by faith, but a faith that is more than mental assent, one that works.

In the area of moral teaching, we must again be careful to note exactly what the Bible is teaching, and the context in which a certain statement is found. For example, it is sometimes said that the Old Testament allows polygamy while the New Testament doesn't, thus creating a contradiciton. While the Old Testament does portray polygamy as practiced even among some of the leading people, it never teaches that this is God's intent for marriage. In the entire realm of ethics, we must consider the fact of progression in the revelation of God and His demands for mankind.

As we move from the Old Testament to the New, man comes into a closer relationship with God and has a greater knowledge of Him; consequently God's demands are higher. This in no way means that God changes His perfect standards. It simply means that

He applies them graciously according to the situation of man. A Father is more apt to treat less severely certain actions by a child who is 5 than he is the same act by a young person who is 18. This does not mean that the act is right in one instance and wrong in the other. It simply indicates that the standard is applied according to the stage of maturity. In the course of biblical history God has done the same thing with man.

One of the greatest stumbling blocks to belief in the inspiration of the Scriptures comes when we encounter certain commands of God regarding the enemies of His Old Testament people. Under His orders, the people of Israel were to destroy totally their enemies in the conquest of the Promised Land (Deut. 20:16-18). We can add to this fact the spirit of vengeance and vindictiveness frequently expressed by God's people against their foes (Pss. 55, 59, 79, 109, 137). Not only do these passages appear to represent immoral actions and attitudes, but they also seem to be in conflict with other teaching, found especially in the New Testament, concerning our responsibility to love our enemies (Luke 6:35-36).

It is not our purpose to discuss all of the aspects of biblical teaching bearing on these issues. Several factors, however, have particular import. Throughout the Scriptures God appears not only as a God of infinite love, but also a God of righteous judgment. There is certainly no change between the Old and New Testaments when we consider the reality of the coming judgment foretold clearly in the New Testament (Rev. 19:11-21). In fact, Jesus spoke more about the eternal destruction of those who refused to come to God than did any of the New Testament writers.

The cries for God's vengeance, which the Psalmist raised against the public enemies of God and His purposes, are only evidence of God's people sharing His concern for righteousness and truth. They point to the time when sin will be put down and righteousness will triumph.

The slaying of the Canaanites is more understandable when we recognize the depth of their depravity. God did not move against them until the cup of their iniquity was full (Gen. 15:16; Lev. 18:24-30). Then, because of the addiction to all forms of gross sin which had thoroughly infected their society, God brought judgment through His people. Professor Arndt describes the situation well:

The Canaanite tribes by their shameless vices had filled the cup of their guilt to overflowing. When the punishment came, it struck all the inhabitants, the women and children included. The fault was not God's; but it lay with those who had trampled underfoot the laws of justice and decency. When men take themselves and their families aboard a ship, sail out upon the ocean for a pleasure trip, and make that ship a place reeking with wickedness and vice, and then all perish in a hurricane which suddenly falls upon them, who is to blame? Will you accuse God for not discriminating between adults and the children? One dreadful aspect of sin is that the woe it produces is like a whirl-pool, whose suction draws every object which is near by to the bottom. . . . That the Canaanitish women were dissolute and instrumental in causing the Israelites to leave the path of truth and purity, that for the children it was better to perish in infancy than to grow up as devotees of idolatry and vice, are points the mere mention of which will suffice here (W. Arndt, *Bible Difficulties*. St. Louis, Concordia Publishing House, 1932, pp. 53-54).

When we consider the full scope of God's moral nature as taught in Scripture, these problem passages fit. They deal with the stern reality of judgment, but they can be called immoral only if we are prepared to assert our own standard of morality over God's.

Historical Problems

We find historical objections to the Bible arising both from outside information and from alleged internal contradictions. Arguments from outside of the Bible generally have come from historical presuppositions against the supernatural rather than any actual data. For example, one objection, assuming the evolution of man and culture, insisted that the first five books of the Bible, known as the Pentateuch, could not be dated from the time of Moses because most people then were illiterate and Moses was unable to write. Then the Code of Hammurabi was discovered, and since it was written about 1728 B.C., objections to Moses' authorship were dropped.

In other cases, because secular history contained no record of peoples or places mentioned in the Bible, these were taken to be mythological. Millar Burrows, an archeologist from Yale, acknowledges the real source of such problems and at the same time indicates their weakness when he says:

> Archaeology has in many cases refuted the views of modern critics. It has shown in a number of instances that these views rest on false assumptions and unreal, artificial schemes of historical development.

One of the most respected archeologists today, the Jewish scholar Nelson Glueck, forthrightly states his findings concerning the historical reliability of Scripture:

> As a matter of fact, however, it may be stated categorically that no archaeological discovery has ever controverted a Biblical reference. Scores of archaeological findings have been made which confirm in clear outline or in exact detail historical statements in the Bible.

With such a record, it would be presumptuous to hold dogmatically that any remaining problems are insolvable.

When we turn to the alleged historical contradictions within Scripture we find again that when all the information is considered, plausible explanations are possible. Variations in the Gospel accounts of the same incident have been the source of problems for many. One of the most popular concerns is Peter's denial and the crowing of the cock. According to Mark's account the cock crew twice (14:30, 72) while Matthew and Luke simply made the statement that before the cock would crow Peter would deny the Lord three times (Matt. 26:34, 74-75; Luke 22:34, 60-61).

There is, however, no direct contradiction here. Matthew and Luke did not say the cock crowed only once as opposed to Mark's twice. They simply referred to the cock crowing. When we remember that "cockcrowing" was a proverbial expression for early morning these accounts can be easily harmonized. According to Mark 13:35 the third of the four Roman night watches was designated the "cock-crowing." But the cock was also apt to crow earlier, from midnight on. Matthew and Luke gave us the main point of Jesus' prediction that Peter would deny the Lord three times before early morning, signalled by the well-known cock-crowing. On the other hand, Mark reported the greater details of Jesus' words. Both accounts are true.

Problems of variation in accounts, such as that of the cockcrow-ing, can generally be solved if we keep certain principles in mind. We must be sure, first of all, that the incidents were really the same, and not similar, but different, events. Secondly, we must re-member that each writer might have been led of the Spirit to bring out a different emphasis, even a different part of a conversation.

Scientific Problems

Most of the scientific problems raised today stem from a so-called scientific approach to reality that rules out the supernatural. Miracles are rejected as myth because they contradict natural laws. When the fact of God is accepted, however, there can be no legiti-mate reason for denying His supernatural intervention where and when He wills. To insist that what the Bible calls demonic activity is really unscientific superstition is to base belief on unproven presuppositions and not on true science.

Probably most conflicts arise between the Bible and the theory of evolution. Since evolution has never been demonstrated scientif-ically, there is no basis to charge the Bible with conclusive error. That evolution is only an unproven theory is recognized not only by Bible-believing scientists but even by many advocates of evolu-tion. Gerald A. Kerkut, who is not a biblical creationist, wrote a book entitled *Implications of Evolution*. (Elmsford, New York: Pergamon Press, 1960). In it he set forth seven fundamental principles of the evolutionary theory. None of these seven, accord-ing to Kerkut, have ever been proven.

Certain isolated statements are sometimes raised as examples of the Bible's lack of accurate scientific knowledge. One of the classic instances is Jesus' statement that the mustard seed "is smaller than all other seeds" (Matt. 13:32). Since botanists know of smaller seeds, it is charged that Jesus stated an error. Aside from the fact that it is difficult to understand how we could harmonize an untruth on the lips of Jesus with His claim to speak truth, this statement, when taken in its setting, makes perfectly good sense. Among the seeds the Jews sowed in their gardens or fields, the mustard seed was generally the smallest. Because of this, it became proverbial to speak of it as the smallest of seeds (Matt. 17:20; Luke 17:6).

Jesus was using this proverbial expression as an illustration of spiritual truth. Only if He were intending to make a scientific statement covering all seeds could His statement be charged with error.

The Absence of the Inerrant Original Manuscripts

A seemingly telling blow against the position of inerrant inspiration is the fact that we do not possess the original writings of Scripture. The Hebrew and Greek manuscripts of Scripture we do possess are not perfect copies of the originals, so we do not have an absolutely inerrant text to point to. Some people claim there is no point in arguing for the infallible, inerrant inspiration of the Bible when we simply do not have such a Bible.

While at first this reasoning may seem quite logical, further thought reveals that it overlooks important facts. In the first place, our belief in inerrant inspiration does not rest ultimately on the fact that we can demonstrate the Bible is without error. It rests on the truth that Christ and the biblical writers taught it.

The belief in the inerrancy of the original writings has value for us even though they have perished. We would all admit that our desk rulers and tape measures are not absolutely accurate. They are close approximations to one degree or another of the master standards maintained by the National Bureau of Standards in Washington. We may not have been aware that such a standard exists; nevertheless, our rulers and tapes have value because they are based on an absolute standard. Similarly, our present Bibles —even with minor flaws—have value because there is an absolute standard behind them.

The belief in original inerrancy is a final control in our search for an absolutely reliable guide to truth. If we believe the original Scriptures were inerrant, then we are free to alter the text of Scripture only in those places where the science of textual studies leads us to believe we can change it to be closer to the original writings. When we do not believe that the original writings were inerrant we are free to accept or reject the Bible at any point we think it to be in error, as judged by some outside standard of truth. The belief in an inerrant original invariably affects our attitude toward, and our use of, our present Bible.

We must not leave this particular objection, however, without pointing out the closeness of our present Bibles to the original texts. We have spoken of certain minor differences in the ancient copies we possess. The great number of copies we have to compare, however, and the general reliability of copyists have made it possible for scholars to virtually ascertain the reading of the original text. One of the leading New Testament scholars, F. F. Bruce, has this to say about the text of the New Testament: "The variant readings about which any doubt remains . . . affect no material question of historic fact or of Christian faith and practice."

Another authority in this field declares, "It cannot be too strongly asserted that in substance the text of the Bible is certain: Especially is this the case with the New Testament. The number of manuscripts of the New Testament, of early translations from it, and of quotations from it in the oldest writers of the Church, is so large that it is practically certain that the true reading of every doubtful passage is preserved in some one or other of these ancient authorities. This can be said of no other ancient book in the world."

Final Considerations

Whenever we face the issue of difficulties in the Bible we must bear in mind several factors. Although there are still unresolved problems, we must not lose sight of the phenomenal accuracy of the Scripture. No comparison is possible between the Scripture and other ancient writings. Eric Sauer focuses on some interesting facts when he notes:

Moses was instructed in all the wisdom of the Egyptians. What preserved him so that when writing the Pentateuch he did not accept the ancient Egyptian chronology which later Manetho laid down definitely in his writings and which was supposed to start 30,000 years before Christ? What influenced Daniel, who was skilled in Chaldean science, to shut his ears to the monstrous Chaldean fables as to the creation of the world? Paul was acquainted with the best science of his time. Why do we find nothing in his speeches or letters similar to Augustine's scornful rejection of the theory of the antipodes, or to the opinion of Ambrose that the sun draws water up to itself that it may thereby cool and refresh itself from its extraordinary heat? (*From Eternity to Eternity,* Grand Rapids: Eerdmans, 1954, p. 106)

Supernatural inspiration is the only way to account for the accuracy of the Bible in all of its 66 books and 1,189 chapters, expecially when we consider the gross errors relating to our world and the divine realm found throughout ancient writings. This should cause anyone to hesitate before calling something he cannot resolve an error.

The number of unresolved problems actually is very small. History shows that as new information comes to light, more and more problems have been solved. It would seem the better part of wisdom to hold an open mind on difficulties that remain rather than act as if we have final truth and charge the Bible with errors. Despite the discoveries of archaeology to date, those who are knowledgeable in this field tell us that only the surface has been scratched compared to what is yet available to examine. In light of the weight of positive evidence for the doctrine of verbal inspiration, it is certainly reasonable to wait for more evidence. Augustine's attitude toward biblical difficulties seems most reasonable. Writing to Jerome he said, "If, here or there, I stumble upon something which seems not to agree with the truth, I make no doubt that either the copy is faulty, or the translator did not express exactly the thought of the original, or that I do not understand the matter."

References

[1]William Arndt, *Does the Bible Contradict Itself?* (St. Louis: Concordia, 1976).

——— *Bible Difficulties* (St. Louis: Concordia, 1957). John W. Haley, *An Examination of the Alleged Discrepancies of the Bible.*

9

The Canon
of Scripture

The word *canon* is derived from a Greek word which meant "a reed." The word suggested a straight rod used as a measuring rule. It came to mean "an authoritative norm" and could be used in a variety of ways. For instance, authoritative standards in ethics, art, or grammar were referred to as canons. Paul used this word for a rule of behavior in Galatians 6:16.

In the early church, *canon* was applied to those writings considered authoritative or part of "the rule of faith." Writings accepted as authoritative for the church were called *canonical* and were included in the collection of writings termed "the canon of Scripture." The first clear application of these words to Scripture was probably by Athanasius, Bishop of Alexandria, around A.D. 350.

When we talk about the canon of Scripture we must understand exactly what we mean. Since the historical process of collecting the 66 books of the Bible involved people, we may think that the people themselves made something canonical. This, however, is not the case. The writings of Scripture are authoritative by virtue of their inspiration. Since they are God's Word, they were canonical as soon as they were written. In accepting these writings as canonical, the people of God were simply recognizing what God had already made canonical. As author James Packer says,

"The Church no more gave us the New Testament canon than Sir Isaac Newton gave us the force of gravity. God gave us gravity, by His work of creation, and similarly He gave us the New Testament canon, by inspiring the individual books that make it up" (J.I. Packer, *God Speaks to Man,* London: Hodder-and Stoughton, 1965, p. 81).

It is true that human judgment was involved in the process. But to say that human judgment is the key element in the establishment of the canon overlooks several truths. First, in order to recognize something as true, one must have something true to recognize. Thus, the assent of God's people to the inspiration of a particular writing does not make it inspired. Its inspiration existed prior to the assent.

Second, this truth is borne out in the actual historical process of "canonization." We never find a church council saying in effect, "We have reviewed this writing and found it to be good; henceforth, it will be considered a part of the canon." Instead of conferring canonicity on a book, the pronouncements were always statements of recognizing what the scattered congregations already considered canonical.

In the face of some perplexity concerning exactly which books were to be received, the pronouncements of the councils said in effect, "These are the books which have always been accepted." The inspiration of the writings by God makes them canonical. They were preserved by the providence of God, and then recognized and received by God's people as being His inspired and sacred Word.

L. Gaussen, who wrote the classic *The Inspiration of the Holy Scriptures* (Chicago: Moody Press, 1949), illustrates the process of the development of the canon by the picture of a woman walking through a garden with its owner. As they stroll along the paths he presents her with one flower after another until he has gathered a whole bouquet for her. The bouquet exists and is admired from the moment that she receives the first flowers. In this same way the canon existed among God's people from the moment that the first inspired writings were given by God. To these first writings, God gave and His people received those additional books which He desired to complete the canon of Scripture.

The Old Testament Canon

We do not have a full historical account of the acceptance of each book in the Old Testament. However, we are given examples in the Scriptures themselves of the reception of writings as canonical which serve to illustrate this action among God's people.

The writings of Moses were immediately accepted as the authoritative words of God, as evidenced in Exodus 24:3: "Then Moses came and recounted to the people all the words of the Lord and all the ordinances; and all the people answered with one voice, and said, 'All the words which the Lord has spoken we will do!' "

Later Joshua's words were written "in the book of the law of God" (Josh. 24:26). Samuel's words were also written in "the book and placed . . . before the Lord" indicating recognition of them as absolutely authoritative words for the community of God's people. Daniel, a young contemporary of Jeremiah, gave evidence that Jeremiah's words were received as the word of God when he wrote, "I, Daniel observed in the books the number of the years which was revealed as the word of the Lord to Jeremiah the prophet . . ." (Dan. 9:2).

It is clear that the people of God recognized the concept of an authoritative canonical word from God, and also that they accepted certain writings as canonical when they were given through God's spokesmen.

The recognition of certain books leads to the further question, what were the criteria the people used in determining that a certain book was canonical? Several suggestions have been proposed by liberal scholars who deny the inspiration of the writings. One determining principle is said to be the age of the writing. If it was ancient, it was canonical. The problem is that other ancient books were not accepted.

Another supposed criterion was that a book was written in the Hebrew language. However, other Hebrew books were not included and certain portions of Daniel and Ezra were not written in Hebrew but in Aramaic.

Still another suggestion is that the writings that agree with the Torah or the books of Moses were considered canonical. While the remainder of the Old Testament certainly does agree with

Moses, the Jews had other writings which were in agreement with the Torah, but were not included in the canon.

Finally, some have suggested that any book of religious value was included in the canon. Again, there are books—in the Apocrypha, for example—which have religious value, just as there are Christian books written today with such value; but these never found their way into the canon of Scripture.

In the final analysis, the answer to the question of certain criteria comes down to the matter of inspiration. Those books considered to be divinely inspired were recognized as canonical by the people.

How did the people know that a particular writing had the quality of inspiration? Two fundamental principles come into play. First was the presence of men and women with a prophetic ministry in the midst of the people. God's people accepted divinely inspired prophets who communicated God's revelation to them. Such leaders authenticated their message by miracles, by true predictions of the future, and by the dynamic nature of their message. A clear example is Moses to whom God gave the ability to work wonders to prove to the people that he was divinely commissioned (cf. Ex. 4:1 ff).

Second, the Spirit of God worked in the midst of the people so that they recognized the voice of God in the words of the prophet. Jesus said, "My sheep hear My voice" (John 10:27). In the time of the Old Testament prophets, just as in Jesus' day, some people did not recognize the voice of God in the prophetic message and therefore as an authoritative norm for their lives. Only through the influence of the Spirit of God were people compelled to accept the sacred writings as the authoritative Word of God.

Undoubtedly, other practical factors came into play at certain points to determine the prophetic nature of a writing. Factual errors naturally exclude some writings. Doctrinal deviations from accepted standards of God's Word would disqualify others. Finally, the acceptance of a book by the original community was important for its recognition later. But these standards all looked to the fundamental criterion—was it truly prophetic and therefore inspired by God?

For the Christian, of course, the final validation of the Old

Testament Scriptures is found in the statements of Christ and the writers of the New Testament. When Jesus mentioned the Law, the Prophets, and the Psalms (Luke 24:44), He was referring to the three divisions of the Hebrew canon which contained the same books as our Old Testament today. These three divisions constituted Scripture, which He held to be absolutely authoritative and thus canonical (John 10:35).

The New Testament writers also taught the inspiration of the entire Old Testament and indicated its authoritativeness by citing from all parts of it. Citations from the Old Testament come from every Old Testament book except Obadiah, Nahum, Ezra, Nehemiah, Esther, Song of Solomon and Ecclesiastes. Nahum and Obadiah, however, were part of one book in the Hebrew canon called The Book of the Twelve Prophets. This book was amply quoted. Ezra and Nehemiah originally formed one book with Chronicles. Esther, Song of Solomon, and Ecclesiastes belong to the group of books known as the Writings, to which the Psalms also belongs. Considering these groupings we can say that the New Testament writers cited from every portion of the Old Testament, giving evidence of their belief in its entire canonicity.

The Development of the Old Testament Canon

The Scriptures have little to say about the actual process of collecting the various canonical books. This is not surprising since the writings were accepted by God's people as they were received. No leading person or council was necessary to make them canonical. Nevertheless, we are given some idea of the gradual development of the canon.

The writings of Moses were immediately accepted and laid the groundwork for a collection of authoritative writings to which further prophetic works were added. The laws of Moses were stored in the tabernacle beside the Ark of the Covenant (Deut. 31:24-26). They were read in the hearing of all the people of Israel (Deut. 31:11) and future kings had a copy of them in order that they might base their decisions on them (Deut. 17:18 ff.).

From this beginning, Moses predicted that future prophets would arise to speak God's word among the people (Deut. 18:15-19). He also gave instructions for judging the prophets in order that false ones might be exposed and rejected (Deut. 13:1-5; 18:20-22). That the people recognized such a chain of prophetic writers is seen in the gradual acceptance of further sacred books. Joshua added his words "in the book of the law of God" (Josh. 24:26), and Samuel "told the people the ordinances of the kingdom, and wrote them in the book and placed it before the Lord" (1 Sam. 10:25). The writers of the Books of Kings and Chronicles were aware of the many prophetic writings covering the entire history of Israel from David to the exile (1 Chron. 29:29; 2 Chron. 9:29). By the time of Daniel, he could refer to "the books" which contained "the prophets" and "the law of Moses" (Dan. 9:2, 6, 11).

Further evidence of a growing canon is seen in the later writers' use of earlier writings, thereby indicating their authoritative character. The books of Moses are cited throughout the Old Testament (Josh. 1:7; 1 Kings 2:3; Mal. 4:4). Joshua is mentioned in Judges (1:1; 2:8). Israel's history from Genesis through Kings is reviewed in Chronicles (1 Chron. 1:1—2:15). Solomon's Proverbs and Songs are mentioned in 1 Kings 4:32, and Daniel refers to Jeremiah (Dan. 9:2). Other references could be cited but these are sufficient to give us some understanding of what took place in the midst of God's Old Testament people as they gradually collected the inspired writings which God gave them.

When the prophetic ministry came to an end, no other writings were added to the canon. The Talmud, which represents ancient Jewish belief, states, "After the latter prophets Haggai, Zechariah, and Malachi, the Holy Spirit departed from Israel." This clearly means that the Spirit no longer provided a prophetic ministry.

The Jewish historian, Josephus, writing during the first century B.C., stated that although records were kept since the time of Artaxerxes (464-424 B.C.), they were not considered equal to the earlier holy writings "because the exact succession of the prophets ceased."

The Extent of the Canon

Beginning with the foundational writings of Moses and continuing with the prophets, the writings of the canon came to be thought of in two great parts—the Law of Moses and the Prophets. This is the predominant way the New Testament speaks of the Old Testament (Matt. 5:17; Luke 16:16, 29, 31; Acts 13:15).

Apparently there was also an early grouping of the books into three parts, a method maintained today in the Hebrew Bible—The Law, The Prophets, and The Writings. The last category includes certain books that were part of the Prophets under the two-fold division. This threefold division also appears to have been known by Christ (Luke 24:44). No one is fully certain of the reason underlying this division but it in no way implies a lesser authority for the Writings since the Psalms are part of this group.

The Old Testament accepted as canonical by the Jews, and later by Christ and the early church, is exactly the same as the 39 books in our present Bibles. Most scholars agree that at first they were arranged in only 24 books. The later Greek translation known as the Septuagint (c. 250-150 B.C.) organized them into only 22 books. These different arrangements, however, simply combined some of the books which are separated in our contemporary Bibles. For instance, 1 and 2 Kings made up only one book.

Not all these writings were always accepted without dispute. At various times, questions were raised about the Song of Solomon, Ecclesiastes, Esther, Ezekiel, and Proverbs. These minor objections, however, never overturned the recognition of these books as canonical.

Many other ancient writings, however, were excluded. These are known as the Pseudepigrapha and the Apocrypha. *Pseudepigrapha* is the name given to a large group of Jewish writings produced between 200 B.C. and A.D. 200. Some of these purport to be written by Adam, Enoch, Moses, and Ezra, hence the title *Pseudepigrapha* or false inscriptions. These books, containing a variety of writings from legendary histories to apocalyptic dreams and visions, were written to sustain the faith of the Jews during a period of unusual suffering. Their false claims to divine authority, along with the fanciful nature of some of the events and some outright false doctrinal teaching, kept the Jews from including them in their canon of sacred Scripture.

The Apocryphal books, numbering 14 or 15, have evoked disagreement over the question of their canonicity. The Roman Catholic Church accepts them as canonical while Jews and Protestants do not. Written between 200 B.C. and A.D. 100 these books mirror with considerable accuracy the religious, political, and social conditions of the years between the Old and New Testaments and provide background for our understanding of certain aspects of the New Testament record.

While some of the early Christian writers appear to quote from these books as authoritative, several reasons preclude us from accepting them as canonical. First, no Hebrew canons of the Old Testament contain these books. Second, while the New Testament writers and Christ quote liberally from the Old Testament, they never cite the Apocrypha as authoritative Scripture. This is especially interesting since the Apostles frequently quoted from the Septuagint, the Greek translation of the Old Testament available at that time. The earliest copies of the Septuagint which we possess (fourth century A.D.) contain the Apocrypha. Whether it was included in New Testament times we do not know. But if it was, the avoidance of it by Jesus and the New Testament writers would be all the more significant.

The third reason for not accepting them as canon is that with a few minor exceptions, all of the lists of the canonical books in the first four centuries exclude these books. Fourth, the contents of the books speak against their canonicity. While they contain much that is true and valuable, doctrinal errors, such as the justification of suicide and prayers for the dead, historical errors, folklore and myth make it impossible to accept them as inspired writings. Moreover, they make no claim to inspiration; in fact, they refer to the absence of prophets in Israel.

For these reasons the church as a whole has never received the Apocrypha as canonical. Its acceptance by the Roman Catholic Church is explained, at least in part, by the fact that the Apocrypha gives support for the Roman belief in prayer for the dead. Such practice is nowhere found in the Jewish and Protestant canons.

The New Testament Canon

The principles for recognition and collection of the Old Testament Scriptures also applied to the New Testament. The main difference was the length of time necessary for acceptance of all the books. The church, rather than being a closely knit community like God's people in the Old Testament, was scattered throughout the world.

The Recognition of the Canonical Writings

The books of the New Testament were written during a brief span of years. For this reason, we have few indications within the Scriptures themselves of the subsequent recognition of a writing. We do find Peter associating the writings of Paul with "other Scriptures" (2 Peter 3:15-16). Paul also may be citing Luke's Gospel as Scripture in 1 Timothy 5:18 (Luke 10:7). Nevertheless, we find that the writings of New Testament men were read publicly in the churches along with the Old Testament Scriptures (1 Thes. 5:27; Col. 4:16; Rev. 1:3; 1 Tim. 4:13).

When we ask by what criterion a particular writing was judged to be authoritative, we are immediately confronted with the concept of apostolic authority in the New Testament church. The Apostles were called by Christ and commissioned by Him to be His authoritative witnesses. As such, they were promised the inspiration of the Spirit who would lead them into truth (John 16:12-16). In their writings they claimed to speak the Word of God by revelation. The church, recognizing the authority of Christ in their teaching, was thus built on the "apostles' teaching" (Acts 2:42; see Eph. 2:20).

The criterion of canonicity was the apostolic identification of a writing. In the case of the few books written by other than apostles, the authors were either known to be closely associated with apostles, as Mark was with Peter, and Luke was with Paul, or the writing clearly expressed apostolic doctrine. In the final sense, a writing was either directly given to the church from the hand of an apostle or imposed upon it by apostolic authority.

The Development of the New Testament Canon

The early churches, spurred by the need to differentiate between false and true writings, moved into the process of selection. Luke wrote his Gospel in order that the true record of Jesus' life might be known; apparently other accounts were circulating (Luke 1:1-4). Paul warned the Thessalonian believers of false letters then in circulation (2 Thes. 2:2). The commands to read and circulate authoritative books also contributed to growing collections of received canonical works. Undoubtedly, copies were made during this process so that different locations could have the same books. Peter's reference to Paul's writings as "other Scriptures" suggests that he had them joined to the Old Testament collections.

In succeeding centuries, we find the earliest Church Fathers supporting the inspiration of all of the books of our New Testament canon. Aside from slight variations—due to the fact that some books were better known in the East or in the West—the translations and canonical lists of the second and third centuries confirm the authority of the same books. With the councils of Hippo (A.D. 393) and Carthage (A.D. 397), the church at large accepted our present 27 books as the canon of the New Testament. Since that time there has never been a serious challenge to the validity of these works either by way of addition or subtraction.

The Extent of the Canon

In the first century A.D., almost 300 other writings related to the church were produced. Their contents are largely heretical and fanciful, and the mainstream of Christianity rejected them, agreeing with Eusebius that these books were "totally absurd and impious." A few other books known as the New Testament Aprocrypha, valuable for devotional and homiletical use, were accepted temporarily in certain limited localities. But they never gained canonical status within the church.

Among the books eventually accepted as the New Testament, seven were in dispute for a time. Some church leaders raised questions about certain teachings in Hebrews, James, 2 Peter, 2 John, 3 John, Jude, and Revelation. In the case of Hebrews, apostolic authorship was uncertain. According to early testimony, however, when the facts about these books were known, all were received as canonical. When these same facts became available to all the church, acceptance quickly followed. By the fourth century after Christ, all 27 books received universal acknowledgement as the Word of God.

10

The Spirit
and the Word

Among books, the Bible stands alone. Other books are from the minds of people to other people. But the Bible is a message from the mind of God to mankind. Through the Scriptures, God Himself speaks to the heart and mind of man. This He does by means of His Spirit who takes the human words and sentences of Scripture and conveys God's message directly to the spirit of man. Theologians refer to this process as the Spirit's work of *illuminating* the Scriptures.

The Need for Illumination

Two great factors make the illuminating work of the Holy Spirit an absolute necessity if we are to understand the Scriptures. The first deals with the nature of the Bible. It is the truth of God, not the thoughts of man. The second relates to the effect of sin on our minds. We may picture our problem as a sharp canyon. On one side is the truth of God in the Scriptures; on the other side is the mind of man. What we need is a bridge to span the gulf that separates the two. That is the work of God Himself through His Holy Spirit.

1. The Spirit knows God. If we are to know God, He must reveal Himself to us. He is not someone or something that human beings can examine and dissect or come to know by reason. God is a Person, and like any person, we cannot really know Him unless He reveals His inner being to us.

In one of the key passages discussing the ministry of the Spirit, Paul spoke of things that our eyes and ears cannot know because they are perceived on a different level and by a means other than our natural senses, namely, "through the Spirit." He then elaborated on the fact that God can be known only through the revealing work of the Spirit. "The Spirit searches all things, even the depths of God. For who among men knows the thoughts of a man except the spirit of the man, which is in him? Even so the thoughts of God no one knows except the Spirit of God. Now we have received . . . the Spirit who is from God, that we might know the things freely given to us by God, which things we also speak . . . in words . . . taught by the Spirit . . ." (1 Cor. 2:10-13).

According to this Scripture, man can not truly know God and His ways unless the Spirit reveals Him. This revelation comes as the Spirit teaches us what the apostles preached. Without the Spirit's ministry the apostles could speak words as the revelation of God, but only the Spirit addresses them to the hearts and spirits of people. For only He is that direct link between the mind of God and the mind of man.

2. *The blindness of sin.* Not only must the Spirit illumine the Word and be its final teacher because He alone knows the mind of God; He must also illumine the Word because of the blinding effect sin has on man. In Eden, before sin entered the world, man needed the Spirit to reveal God's truths to his heart. But with the entrance of sin an additional need for the Spirit's work arose. According to the Bible, people untouched by the Spirit's work are totally unreceptive to God's truth. They are "darkened in their understanding, excluded from the life of God, because of the ignorance that is in them, because of the hardness of their heart" (Eph. 4:18). They do not receive the things of God, and even consider them foolish, till they accept the Spirit's illuminating work (1 Cor. 2:14).

Added to the blinding effect of sin is the deliberate work of Satan who clouds the eyes of the unsaved. Paul wrote, "And even if our Gospel is veiled, it is veiled to those who are perishing, in whose case the god of this world [Satan] has blinded the minds of the unbelieving that they might not see the light of the Gospel of the glory of Christ" (2 Cor. 4:3-4). Without the work of the Spirit the message of the Scriptures cannot penetrate this veil. Human words alone cannot do it. Only God by His Spirit can shine His truth through this darkness.

The saved person is different. The new birth includes the ability to see spiritual things. Nevertheless, the presence of sin creates a blinding effect on him. Using another metaphor, Paul said that believers at Corinth were unable to receive the teaching of "solid food." He had to give them baby's milk because of sin in their lives (1 Cor. 3:1-3). In a similar way, the writer to the Hebrews claimed that the believers to whom he wrote were "dull of hearing" because of sin (Heb. 5:11-14).

Thus the ministry of the Spirit in the illumination of the Word is necessary both for unbelievers and believers. We came to Christ as the Spirit illumined the saving truth to our hearts and we continue to grow in this truth only through the same work of the Spirit. Only He can overcome the dulling effect of sin in our lives.

The Work of Illumination

When we speak of the illuminating ministry of the Spirit, we are entering an extremely important area of truth and yet one that remains somewhat mysterious. Revelation and inspiration deal with the communication of God's truth to us objectively; illumination is concerned with the subjective revelation and application of the Word to our own hearts and minds. To some extent, the actions of God directed to our innermost being will always remain beyond our understanding. Who can explain, for example, the work of the Spirit in the new birth? Nevertheless, the Scriptures do give us some fundamental truths concerning this ministry of the Spirit with the Word and these are essential for our understanding.

1. The definition of illumination. We may define illumination as the work of the Holy Spirit by which He causes the Scriptures to be understood. Some theologians argue that this ministry is only for believers. But it is this same work of the Spirit that causes a person to understand the message of salvation and to come to Christ for salvation. Illumination of the Christian is simply the continued work of the Spirit in which He causes us to grow as we understand how the Word applies to our lives.

We can gain further understanding of the illumination of the Word when we relate it to revelation and inspiration. Revelation concerns the unveiling or making known of God's truth. Inspiration makes possible the accurate statement of that truth in human language. Prophets and apostles, under the ministry of the Spirit, communicated God's truth to others. In both revelation and inspiration, however, the truth of God remains objective to us. That is, it confronts us as something outside of us. In illumination, the Holy Spirit takes the Word and speaks it directly to the human heart. Calvin put it strikingly when he said that the same Spirit who "spake by the mouths of the prophets" must "penetrate into our hearts" and, as it were, repeat the message to us.

One further facet of our definition deserves some emphasis here, namely, that the Spirit illuminates Scripture. From time to time through the history of the church, self-proclaimed spokesmen for God arise, claiming to be enlightened by the Spirit, and preach some new truth not found in the written Word. Often these "prophets" base their claim to inspiration on Paul's contrast between the "letter" and the "spirit" (2 Cor. 3), regarding the letter, taken as the words of Scripture, as inferior to the truth revealed by the Spirit directly to the heart.

Such a separation could not be further from the Apostle's meaning. Throughout the pages of Scripture the apostles tie the ministry of the Spirit to the Word. The Spirit brought the Word into existence as He moved the human authors to write God's words (2 Peter 1:21). He is only being consistent with Himself when He takes this same truth given by inspiration and teaches it by illumination to the hearts of men. It is the Word of God which is the sword of the Spirit (Eph. 6:17). The Word is His instrument in the miracle of the new birth (James 1:18; 1 Peter 1:23) and the sanctification of God's people (John 17:17). Since Christ is the theme of Scripture, the Holy Spirit illumines Scripture in such a way as to reveal Him in all of His glory.

2. The nature of illumination. The act of the Spirit's illumination of the Word for an individual begins in the process of conversion. The natural man without the Spirit's work cannot understand the Bible. He can read it and even repeat its message, but he cannot make sense of it. The prophet Isaiah described such a condition when he wrote, "You have seen many things but you do not observe them; your ears are open, but none hears" (Isa. 42:20). When Paul preached the Gospel, it was a stumbling block to many Jews and foolishness to Gentiles (1 Cor. 1:23). The reason for this reaction, according to the Apostle, lies in the fact that these words are taught by the Spirit, and without Him a person simply cannot "accept the things of the Spirit of God" (1 Cor. 2:14). In the process of conversion the Spirit of God removes the veil blinding the eyes of the heart and speaks the truth of the Gospel to a person so that he sees what it really is.

This same ministry of the Spirit continues with the believer as he grows in the knowledge of God through the Word. The Apostle said the believer is instructed "not in words taught by human wisdom, but in those taught by the Spirit" (1 Cor. 2:13). As a result of the Spirit's teaching the believer has "the mind of Christ" (v. 16).

One of the most provocative passages dealing with the illumination of the Spirit is found in the First Epistle of John. Religious teachers known later as Gnostics, exalted *knowledge* as the way of salvation. They believed that they held the key to knowledge and those who wanted it had to get it from their exclusive teaching. John responded to this teaching by insisting that all believers have received "an anointing from the Holy One" (1 John 2:20). He was thinking of God's gift of the Holy Spirit who belongs to everyone who has placed his faith in Christ. As a result, John told his readers, "you have no need for anyone to teach you; but as this anointing teaches you about all things . . . you abide in Him" (v. 27).

Some Christians, mishandling this passage, have taken the unbiblical position of refusing all human teachers. "We don't need anyone to teach us," they say. "We are taught directly by the Spirit." Such a position ignores the biblical evidence that God has placed gifted teachers within the church. John was not instructing us to disdain all teachers. He was simply saying that we are not totally dependent on the instruction of human teachers for the truth of God. Teachers help us to understand the Word, but it is the Spirit who finally impresses its truth on our minds and hearts.

Apparently, there were some, whom John described as "antichrists," who were teaching things contrary to the truth about the person of Christ (1 John 2:18-23). John responded by insisting that the believer can know the truth about who Christ is because he possesses the Spirit whose business it is to glorify the true Christ to His people (see John 16:14).

Michael Green tells of a soldier who came to Christ under his ministry. Almost immediately the young man was sent to North Africa. Green had no time to teach him the basic biblical truths of the faith. Some months later, however, word came back that this young soldier had organized a Bible study in his quarters. Not only his peers were attending but even high-ranking officers. In this instance, without the aid of human teachers, this believer was taught by the Spirit the knowledge of the Scriptures, sufficiently even to lead others to that same truth.

What, specifically is it that the Spirit does in this ministry? Does His illumining work give us the true interpretation of difficult passages? Does His witness take the place of our own diligent study? In reply to these questions, the Scriptures reveal several fundamental aspects of the illumining work of the Spirit.

First, He gives the ability to understand the meaning of the Scriptures. By this we do not mean that someone without the Spirit is completely unable to give a correct interpretation of what the Scripture says. Many unbelievers have thrown light on the Bible. Their scholarly research into historical backgrounds and the meanings of Hebrew and Greek words are often invaluable in arriving at the true meaning of a text. The Spirit does not give intellectual understanding so much as He does moral understanding. To put it another way, the Spirit gives meaning to the heart and not simply to the head. The problem of the person lacking this ministry of the Spirit is not that he cannot understand the words on the pages of the Bible; it is, rather, that they do not make good sense to him. He cannot grasp their meaning for himself. Instead of ringing true, they appear to be foolishness.

We may illustrate this concept by the words of a loving parent who forbids his youngster to play with a gun or to eat too many sweets. The words of the parents are perfectly clear and understandable to the child. The problem is that the youngster does not perceive them as true and, consequently, rejects them. Later, however, when the child matures, he not only sees the truthfulness and the significance of his parent's words, but usually finds himself giving the same instructions to his own children. Just so, the Scriptures teach that man, unaided by the Spirit, will never truly understand the message of Scripture or appropriate it to himself.

The illumination of the Spirit, therefore, does not take the place of study. We are exhorted to be diligent in "handling accurately the word of truth" (2 Tim. 2:15) and the Bible commends the careful examination of its meaning (Acts 17:11). But diligent study without the ministry of the Spirit can never create true understanding of the message of the Word.

A *second* aspect of the Spirit's illumination is the evernewness of the Scripture. The Psalmist prayed, "Open my eyes, that I may behold wonderful things from Thy law" (Ps. 119:18). The amazing thing about the Scriptures that sets them apart from all other writings is that one can read and reread them and each time glimpse some new facet of truth. They are like a boundless mine out of which one may continually discover new treasures. These treasures, however, are garnered only by the eye that has been opened by God through the Spirit. Sometimes, when we hear the Bible taught by someone who has spent years in its study, we are amazed at the insights that come from a passage, often one we have read over and over. Such additional insights and their applications to life come to the one who spends time as a student of the divine Teacher of the Word, the Holy Spirit.

The *third* aspect of illumination is that the Spirit's ministry always focuses on the theme of Scripture and its purpose for our lives. Jesus declared that all of the Scriptures spoke of Him (John 5:39). Thus, as the Spirit illuminates Scripture, He continually sheds light on the Saviour and His work. It is He who shines "in our heart to give the light of the knowledge of the glory of God in the face of Christ" (2 Cor. 4:6).

Christ promised that the Spirit would glorify Him and witness to Him (John 16:14; 15:26). The reason for this is clear. The purpose of Scripture is that we might come to know God, who has revealed Himself in the Person and work of Christ. Thus, the Spirit's illumining ministry completes this revelation within our minds and hearts. Practically, this focus of the Spirit means that when we are taught by the Spirit, we will not come to know the Scriptures primarily as a history of God's ancient people or even as a book of theological truths, but as a revelation of God Himself in Christ (see Eph. 1:16-17).

The import of this revealing ministry is that we may know how to walk with God. The Psalmist's desire to see "wonderful things" from the Word was bound up with his purpose to "live and keep" God's Word (Ps. 119:17-18). Similarly, the Apostle's prayer for the believers at Colossae was: "that you may be filled with the knowledge of His will in all spiritual wisdom and understanding, so that you may walk in a manner worthy of the Lord" (Col. 1:9-10). The purpose of knowledge gained through illumination of the Scriptures by the Spirit is always obedience of life.

3. *The result of illumination.* The culminating result of the Spirit's ministry of illumining the Word to our hearts and minds is that we come to have the knowledge of God. A "full assurance of understanding" which comes only by the Spirit results "in a true knowledge of God's mystery, that is, Christ Himself" (Col. 2:2). John similarly said, "And we know that the Son of God has come, and has given us understanding in order that we might know Him who is true" (1 John 5:20).

So intimately is this knowledge of God tied to the Word that the Scriptures speak of the Word coming to reside in the believer. James spoke of the "implanted" Word (1:21) that someone has described as "the Word deeply rooted within you." It is the abiding presence of the indwelling Word that marks a person off as a Christian (1 John 1:8, 10; 2:4). Thus, the indwelling Word by the ministry of the Spirit and the true knowledge of God are one and the same. The German Reformation leader, Martin Luther reflected this union when he wrote:

Since these promises of God are holy, true, righteous, free, and peaceful words, full of goodness, the soul which clings to them with a firm faith will be so closely united with them and altogether absorbed by them that it not only will share in all their power but will be saturated and intoxicated by them. If a touch of Christ healed, how much more will this most tender spiritual touch, this absorbing WORD of God, communicate to the soul all things that belong to the Word ("The Freedom of a Christian," *Luther's Works,* XXXI, 349).

The Reception of Illumination

Illumination of the Scriptures does not happen automatically. It requires that we follow God's instruction for the reception of this ministry of the Spirit. These instructions involve our attitude and our actions.

1. *Attitude of humble faith.* "God is opposed to the proud, but gives grace to the humble" (James 4:6). The revelation of the true meaning of the Bible is an act of God's grace that we can only experience in humble submission. Anyone who believes that he is wise or who wants to gain the wisdom of Scripture simply through academic means will never experience the teaching ministry of the Spirit. God hides His truth from the "wise and intelligent" and reveals it to "babes" (Luke 10:21). A humble attitude of faith is evident in the Psalmist who did not look to himself for understanding but prayed to God: "Open my eyes" (Ps. 119:18); "teach me, O Lord. . . . Give me understanding" (vv. 33-34).

2. *Obedience to the light received.* Growth in the knowledge of Scripture under the divine tutelage of the Spirit depends on our obedience to what He has already given to us. The tragedy of many in Jesus' day was their self-righteousness. They had turned from the light they had received. As a consequence, Jesus taught in parables so that his disciples, who wanted to know God's truth, could receive it, and those who had refused to respond to previous revelation were blinded (Matt. 13:13-16).

Christians today can also become dull to the Spirit's teaching by choosing to walk after the things of the flesh. A church member once remarked with a note of pride that he had been through the Bible five times that year. His pastor lovingly responded, "How often has the Bible been through you?" A serious effort to live by one commandment of Scripture will result in more true knowledge than reading it through without any effort to obey it.

3. *Meditation on the Scripture.* Growth in true knowledge of the Scriptures comes only as we spend time exposing ourselves to its truth and actively meditating on its words. The Psalmist declared, "I shall delight in Thy commandments, which I love. . . . I will meditate on Thy statutes. O how I love Thy law! It is my meditation all the day. My eyes anticipate the night watches, that

I may meditate on Thy word" (Ps. 119:47-48, 97, 148).

The various approaches of people to the study of Scripture have been aptly illustrated by the actions of a butterfly, a botanist and a bee. The butterfly alights for a moment or two on a beautiful flower and then flits off to another, touching many but deriving little benefit from them. The botanist spends time over each flower, examining it carefully, making copious notes in his notebook. When he is finished he closes the notebook and sets his mind to other things, leaving most of his information in the closed pages. But the bee comes along, spending time in each flower. He finally emerges from the garden, loaded with pollen and nectar.

In a similar way some people flit here and there in the Bible, hitting a few favorite verses but getting little out of them. Others study diligently, cataloging facts and doctrines in their intellect but not really allowing the Spirit to teach their heart. But some are like the bee. They spend time in the Word, reading and meditating so that it fills their minds with the wisdom from above till it comes to guide their walk in the paths of life.

11

The Power of the Word

When Jesus was tempted by the devil to turn stones into bread and assuage His hunger, He replied, "Man shall not live on bread alone, but on every word that proceeds out of the mouth of God" (Matt. 4:4). This truth, given centuries earlier through Moses (Deut. 8:3), highlights the central quality of the Word of God— it is alive with the power and dynamic of God. As such, it is the instrument through which God makes known His will in the world.

This fact has always given the Bible its unique place in the lives and hearts of God's people. It is not simply another book; it is the Book which, according to the Lord Himself, is absolutely necessary for life.

This thought immediately raises many questions. How can mere words, written on pages of paper, live? How do they communicate life? What do they accomplish? These questions are of vital importance in our attitude toward and use of Scripture in our daily lives.

The Vitality of the Word
In the well-known parable of the sower, Jesus likened the Word of God to seed (Luke 8:11). A dry grain of wheat or kernel of corn may look uncomplicated. In fact, it would undoubtedly be

possible for someone to produce artificial wheat or corn so that it could not be distinguished from the real thing simply by looking at and handling it. The true test, however, is in planting it in the ground. Living seed produces a living plant while the fake one disintegrates into the soil.

Just so, the Bible may appear as any other book, but when it is received it has the amazing power to produce spiritual life. Following the same seed image of Jesus, James wrote, "Receive the Word implanted, which is able to save your souls" (James 1:21). The Word is God's seed bearing within itself a life principle even as seeds do on a natural level.

The living quality of the Word is expressly declared by the writer to the Hebrews: "For the Word of God is living and active and sharper than any two-edged sword, and piercing as far as the division of soul and spirit, of both joints and marrow, and able to judge the thoughts and intentions of the heart" (Heb 4:12). Interestingly, the word *living* is applied by the same author frequently to God Himself (Heb. 3:12; 9:14; 10:31; 12:22). He is the "living God" who sends His Word forth with His life.

Because it is "living," the Word is also "active." The Greek word *energes* is related to our English words "energy" and "energetic" and denotes something powerfully active and effective. The same word in its verb form is used of God working in us to accomplish His will (Phil. 2:13). Thus, just as the life of God comes to us through the reception of the Word, so God's energy and power are at work in us through His Word.

Jesus taught that His words were also the words of His Father in heaven (see John 17:14). He said, "the words that I have spoken to you are spirit and are life" (John 6:63). On this occasion, many who had followed Jesus turned away to walk with Him no more. But the disciples had received the words of Jesus and experienced their power. When asked if they too would leave, Peter, who undoubtedly spoke for all of them, responded, "Lord, to whom shall we go? You have words of eternal life" (6:68).

In a stinging indictment against the false prophets who speak their own words and give the people not "the slightest benefit" (Jer. 23:32), God proclaimed the power of His true Word. "Is not My Word like fire . . . and like a hammer which shatters a rock?" (v. 29) To the prophet Jeremiah, He declared, "Behold I am making My words in your mouth fire and this people wood, and it will consume them" (Jer. 5:14). When Jeremiah refused for a time to speak the Word God gave him, he testified of this same effect in his "heart" and in his "bones" as the Word became "like a burning fire" (Jer. 20:9).

Contrary to the images of fire and hammer, which suggest the destructive power of the Word, Isaiah saw the productive elements of nature as illustrations of the effective power of the Word. In the context of salvation, God said through the prophet, "For as the rain and the snow come down from heaven, and do not return there without watering the earth, and making it bear and sprout, and furnishing seed to the sower and bread to the eater; so shall My Word be which goes forth from My mouth; it shall not return to Me empty, without accomplishing what I desire, and without succeeding in the matter for which I sent it" (Isa. 55:10-11).

These statements about the living and dynamic qualities of the Word must not be understood to mean that the Word is only living at certain times when God by His Spirit chooses to make it so. Nowhere in these Scriptures do we find the suggestion that the Word is only dynamic on certain occasions. To be sure, the effect of the living Word is not always evident. But this is due to human failure to receive it. The fact that a seed must be planted in order to produce fruit in no sense negates the life of the seed. Moreover, as we shall see, even when the Word of God is ignored and rejected it will still have its effect in the day of judgment.

Salvation through the Word

If the Word of God does come into our midst with the living power of God Himself, it is only fitting that we find it employed in His great purpose of salvation. Just as Christ, the personal Word of God, came to seek and to save the lost, so the Scriptures are the instrument for the communication of this salvation to men. Two things are essential for salvation—the knowledge of the Gospel and faith to receive it. Both are given through the revelation of God in the Scriptures.

1. The Gospel through the Word. The place of the Word in the salvation plan of God is expressly stated by the Apostle Paul. Writing to the Corinthians he said, "God was well-pleased through the foolishness of the message preached to save those who believe" (1 Cor. 1:21). Comparing salvation to purification, Jesus likewise taught His disciples that the Word was the means by which we are saved. "You are already clean," He told them, "because of the Word which I have spoken to you" (John 15:3).

The place of the Word in salvation is highlighted in Scripture by the appeals God makes that men might listen to Him. In Isaiah, we find God calling out, "Listen carefully to Me, and eat what is good. . . . Incline your ear and come to Me. Listen, that you may live" (Isa. 55:2-3). God has ordained His salvation to come through the hearing of His Word. Only the Scriptures are able to "give you the wisdom that leads to salvation" (2 Tim. 3:15).

The effectiveness of the Word of God in producing salvation explains the many attempts of the enemy to eliminate the Bible. In the last great persecution of Christians before Christianity became a legal religion in the Roman Empire, Roman authorities were considering ways to crush Christianity once and for all. When an apostate Christian in the emperor's council heard them speak of burning all of the Christians, he responded, "It is no use to burn the Christians, for if you burn every Christian alive today, and leave a single copy of the Scriptures remaining, the Christian church will spring up again tomorrow." Whereupon the emperor issued a decree ordering the destruction of the Scriptures.

The Scriptures are the means of salvation because they reveal the Good News of God's saving acts in Christ. Paul pointed to this power when he testified to the Romans, "For I am not ashamed of the Gospel, for it is the power (*dunamis*, as in our "dynamite") of God for salvation to everyone who believes" (Rom. 1:16).

In the narrow sense, the Gospel focuses on the death of Christ for our sins and His triumphant resurrection (1 Cor. 15:1-4). In a broader sense, however, the whole of Scripture, including the revelation of our sinful condition and God's solution, may be said to be the Gospel. For apart from the light of God's Word exposing our lost estate, the revelation of the work of Christ would be meaningless. Thus, the Bible totally is God's Word. He plants it as a spiritual seed into the hearts of those who receive it.

2. *Faith through the Word.* We may be tempted to say, "Yes, the Word is the life-giving seed because of the message it con-

tains, but the seed must be received. What we need is something to incite our faith to receive the Word." Again, however, the living Word is God's ordained instrument for this work. The Holy Spirit, to be sure, prepares hearts and opens the eyes of faith in the Word, but He does this through the Word, even as the Apostle declared, "So faith comes from hearing and hearing by the Word of Christ" (Rom. 10:17).

Only as we expose ourselves to the Word and allow the illumining work of the Spirit to lift the veil from our eyes do we find faith in the living Word. Only as we gaze on the truth of the Word, which is finally the Person of the Saviour, and allow the Spirit to glorify Him before us, will we commit ourselves to Him.

Since God uses the Word to incite faith, its use in evangelistic efforts is absolutely imperative. Some friends of Ralph C. Norton, the Director of Personal Work for the Chapman-Alexander Mission, noticed that he used the Bible almost exclusively in his personal witnessing. "What do you do," they asked, "when an unsaved person does not accept the Bible as having any authority?" Mr. Norton responded, "Well, if I had a fine Damascus sword with a keen double-edged blade I would not sheath it in a fight just because the other man said he did not believe it would cut."

This is not to suggest that studying evidence for the reliability of the Bible is of no value. Reasons for believing the Bible can often help someone hear the truth of Scripture. But we must always remember that "the sword of the Spirit" is not our words —even our arguments. It is, rather, the Word of God. The Spirit uses the light of Scripture to penetrate the darkness of human minds (Eph. 6:17).

A bright physician discovered this in an encounter with D.L. Moody. He admitted that he went to hear Mr. Moody only for laughs. "I knew he was not a scholar, and I felt sure I could find many flaws in his argument. But I found that I could not get at the man. He just fired one Bible text after another at me till they went home to my heart straight as bullets from a rifle. I tell you, Moody's power is in the way he has his Bible at the tip of his tongue."

Christian Growth through the Word
The Word is not only active in bringing us to Christ; it is also

the means of our growth in Christ. The testimony of an old Scottish Christian finds an echo in every believer's heart. "I have a most depraved and sinful nature," he said, "and do what I will, I find I cannot make myself holy. My friends cannot do it for me, nor do I think an angel in heaven could. One thing alone does it—reading and believing what I read in that blessed Book; that does it."

Jesus pointed to this truth when he said to the Tempter: "Man shall not live on bread alone, but on every word that proceeds out of the mouth of God" (Matt. 4:4). As physical food is essential for physical growth, so the Word is necessary for spiritual growth.

In His prayer for His people, Jesus asked the Father, "Sanctify them in the truth; Thy Word is truth" (John 17:17). Later, Peter likened the nourishing value of the Word to milk for babies. After teaching that the believer is born into the Christian life through the Word, (1 Peter 1:23), he added, "like newborn babes, long for the pure milk of the Word, that by it you may grow in respect to salvation" (2:2). Christian growth requires that we feed on the same Word that brought us life.

Paul summarized this effect of the Word on the believer, calling it "profitable for teaching, for reproof, for correction, for training in righeousness; that the man of God may be adequate, equipped for every good work" (2 Tim. 3:16-17).

The implications of this truth are tremendous, both in individual and church practice. Because of its power, Paul exhorted the Colossian believers to "let the Word of Christ richly dwell within you . . ." (Col. 3:16). When we go on in this passage, we see the effects of the indwelling Word. We find that they are similar to those of the Spirit-filled life (see Eph. 5:18-20). This makes sense because we know that the Spirit works through the Word. It is not only His sword against our spiritual enemies (Eph. 6:17); it is also His means for our growth. Thus Paul could commit his fellow believers at Ephesus to the highest possible good for their lives, namely, "to God and to the Word of His grace, which is able to build you up and give you the inheritance among all those who are sanctified" (Acts 20:32).

The Scriptures not only teach their power to promote spiritual growth; they also suggest the specific ways this is accomplished.

Jesus said they are effective because they are truth (John 17:17). The Bible is not some magical book that creates wonderful results simply because we carry it around or read it. Our reading must be with understanding. Scripture is effective only as we understand and appropriate it.

It would be impossible, however, to list all the facets of the truth God has revealed to us in Scripture. The study of the person of our Saviour alone is inexhaustible. There are, however, two great fundamental themes revealed in Scripture which summarize the truth involved in spiritual growth: (1) the revelation of our sin, and (2) the revelation of the Saviour. Obviously, these are the same truths we encounter in becoming a Christian. Growth in the Christian life, then, is simply allowing the basic truths to express their power in our lives by faith.

1. The Word reveals sin. In the revelation of sin, the Word discloses the righteous standards of God and our failure to live by them. The psalmist declared, "How can a young man keep his way pure? By keeping it according to Thy Word" (Ps. 119:9). James likened the Word to a mirror in which we can see ourselves just as we are. Etched on this mirror is God's standard, the "perfect law" to show us our defects (James 1:23-25).

While the metaphor of the mirror suggests an inactive reflector, the writer of Hebrews declares that the Word actively exposes us. It leaves nothing hidden. Describing the Word as "living and active and sharper than any two-edged sword," he declares that the living Word penetrates to the depths of our being including the judging of "the thoughts and intentions of the heart" (Heb. 4:12). As a result of the Word's activity, "all things are open and laid bare to the eyes of Him with whom we have to do" (v. 13). A Chinese man, after hearing the Bible for the first time, said to the missionary, "I know this is God's Word because it tells me all that I am."

We see the exposing effect of the Word on the believer in the experience of Peter. On the night of Jesus' arrest, immediately following Peter's third and final denial of his Lord, "the Lord turned and looked at Peter. And Peter remembered the word of the Lord" (Luke 22:61). In this case it was the specific word predicting his denial, but the principle applies throughout. It is the Word of God which causes the believer to see his sin and turn from it in repentance. The Psalmist declared, "The Law of the Lord is perfect, restoring the soul" (19:7).

2. *The Word reveals the Saviour.* It is one thing to see God's Holy standard in the Scriptures and be convicted of our failure to match it, but it is quite another matter to be able to do something about it. One evening at the dinner table, our daughter pointed out to me that my nose was not straight. This was not exactly a new revelation. The mirror has shown me that consistently. The problem is that there is not too much that I can do about it. Our problem with sin is much the same. The Bible reveals that all men are sinners and fall short of God's pattern for life. But as beneficial as that revelation of ourselves may be, it does no good unless we find some means of change.

The Bible, however, is more than a revelation of God's standard and a mirror of our failure. It contains the message of God's great work of redemption through Christ. When the Apostle called the Gospel "the power of God for salvation," he was not simply referring to the initial coming to Christ for eternal life. *Salvation* means "wholeness or soundness." And that is what God has in mind for us.

By the Gospel we begin the Christian life and by the same Gospel we grow. When Paul wanted to stimulate the believers at Rome to sanctification and spiritual growth, he asked them to remember what happened in their initial salvation (Rom. 6:1-11). They had died with Christ and were resurrected to newness of life in Him. Their sins were forgiven and they were new creatures.

According to the Apostle, the key to growth is to consider the great facts of the Gospel and to live according to them. To put it very practically, the Scriptures declare that we are to appropriate daily by faith the truth of the Gospel. We are free from the bondage of sin, our sins are forgiven, and by the Holy Spirit we live the resurrection life of Christ. This gracious redemption is the theme of the Scriptures. As we read the Scriptures, therefore, the Spirit of God shines His illumining Word in our minds and hearts again and again, and incites renewed faith to live by it.

A striking illustration of the cleansing and renewing power of the Word is found in the Old Testament ordinance of the red heifer (Num. 19). According to the law of Moses, one who had been defiled had to be purified before he could again resume his place in society. For the purpose of cleansing any defilement, a red heifer was taken outside the camp of Israel and slain. Some of its blood was then sprinkled in front of the tent of meeting seven times as a sacrifice to the Lord. After this, the animal was burned totally to ashes which were gathered up and mixed with water referred to as "water to remove impurity" (v. 9). When the Children of Israel were defiled, this water was applied to them and they were cleansed.

The effectiveness of the water lay in the fact that the water contained the ashes of a sacrificial death. Every time it was applied the benefits of that death were made present again. So it is with the Scriptures. They contain the sacrificial work of Christ for our cleansing (see Eph. 5:26). The blood sprinkled once for all at Calvary brings the believer into relationship with God. But as we walk in this life we get defiled. We need the repeated application of the truth of Christ's triumph over sin and our newness of life in Him. This message is brought to us in the Word. As we read and meditate on it, the Spirit of God uses it as a water of purification for our lives.

In addition to revealing the Saviour as the one who cleanses our lives, the Scriptures also reveal the matchless perfection of His Person. He is our Head and Pattern; we are to be conformed to His image (Rom. 8:29). The process of our conformation to Christ was outlined by the Apostle Paul in 2 Corinthians 3:18 where he explained, "But we all, with unveiled face beholding as in a mirror the glory of the Lord, are being transformed into the same image from glory to glory, just as from the Lord, the Spirit." The place of Scripture in this process is in the revelation of the glory of Christ. By His own testimony He is the theme of all Scripture (John 5:39). As the Spirit illumines the Scriptures, He shines the spotlight on Christ and glorifies Him before us (John 16:14). When we behold Him, the Apostle says, we are gradually "transformed into the same image."

We all know that when we spend extended periods of time with a person whom we respect and admire, we begin to take on certain traits of that person. This process is all the more effective when we spend time with Christ through meditation on the Scriptures. In this way the power of the Spirit of God works in us to conform us to Him.

The revelation of Christ is certainly a major explanation of the Psalmist's words, "Thy Word have I treasured in my heart that I may not sin against Thee" (Ps. 119:11). There is no greater power for the prevention of sin in our lives than the image of our Lord constantly in our minds through consistent time spent in the Word.

Judgment through the Word

Jesus declared that He did not come "to judge the world, but to save the world" (John 12:47; see also John 3:17). Nevertheless, His coming with the light of God brought judgment to those who rejected Him (John 3:19). The Word of God has this same double effect. We have seen its power to save and nourish spiritual life, but we cannot conclude this chapter without also noting the power of the Word to judge. Jesus said, "He who rejects me, and does not receive My sayings, has One who judges him; the Word I spoke is what will judge him at the last day" (John 12:48). The Apostle Paul likewise viewed his ministry of the Word as an aroma "from life to life" for those who received it, but one "from death to death" for those who spurned it (2 Cor. 2:15-17).

The Word brings judgment and death because its living power forces on a person the decision either to receive or resist its message. Continued resistance brings a hardening which ends in death. We can compare the activity of the Word to that of the sun. Certain materials soften and melt under the rays of the sun, while others harden. So with the Word; to some it brings conviction and repentance, to others hardening and final judgment.

Paul's Charge

The implications of the power of the Word are pointedly made in Paul's charge to young Timothy: "Preach the Word" (2 Tim. 4:2). The Word is the "sword of the Spirit," but it is not only to be His weapon. We are told to "take . . . the sword of the Spirit," in our hands and use it. The power of the Spirit is there, but it must be wielded by us. If we would take seriously the biblical teaching on the dynamic of the Scriptures, they must become central both in our contacts with the unsaved and in the practice of our Christian lives, personally and together in the church.

12

The Use
of the Bible

Studying the doctrine of the Word of God is of little value unless it leads to the practical use of the Scriptures in life. In this final chapter we want to focus on three important essentials for implementing in our experience the truth we have seen thus far. If Scripture is to be personally relevant we must first respect it for what it is—the Word of Almighty God which speaks authoritatively and sufficiently to all of life. Second, we must seek to understand what it really says and not impose our own thoughts on it. Finally, we must hear the Word, which in the biblical sense means to heed and obey it.

Respecting God's Word
In the course of life we receive communications from various sources. Our children, for example, ask us for things; our bosses make demands. We try to consider every communication given in good faith. But whether we respond to the demand or not depends, in part, on who issues the message. If the one speaking to us has authority over us and if his word concerns us personally, we sit up and take notice. If, on the other hand, we recognize no authority in the speaker, we often feel free to make our own decision about the matter.

The same principle is at work in the Scriptures. Only when we respect them for what they are can we properly obey them.

1. The Authority of the Bible. We all defer to some ultimate authority when we make decisions. It may be our own personal feelings, it may be the opinion of some group we respect, or it may be a supernatural revelation.

Among many professing believers today it is popular to look to one's own experience as the final criterion of what is authoritative in Scripture. The Bible may say something to one person, but remain silent to another. Each person is somehow given a private meaning, authoritative for them alone.

Such a position is in reality a denial of the absolute authority of Scripture. If the Bible delivers different truths to different people, it speaks no truth at all. Truth implies the opposite of falsity. But if each person's opinion is correct there is no falsity and thus no truth. Such a personal source of truth is in reality finding truth within ourselves and reading it into Scripture.

Speaking of morality, C. S. Lewis once observed that man is incapable of establishing ultimate standards. "The human mind," he said, "has no more power of inventing a new value than of planting a new sun in the sky or a new primary color in the spectrum." The same can be said of truth. As finite creatures, we cannot be the source of ultimate truth.

A second way of understanding the authority of the Bible is to view it through the opinion of the community of professing believers or the church. This has been the traditional position of the Roman Catholic Church. Catholic writer Karl Adam in *The Spirit of Catholicism* declares, "the Bible possesses no independent authority apart from the church."

This same position is extolled today by some liberal Protestant scholars. Having surrendered belief in the full inspiration and authority of the Bible, they look to the experience of the church as the final arbiter of truth. What the church at any point in history teaches as the voice of God is true. Thus, the Scriptures no longer stand over the church as God's authoritative Word. Instead, the church stands over the Scriptures to declare what is or is not normative. In the final sense, this position has the same source of truth as the first, namely the human mind. Only in this case it is a community of minds rather than the individual.

Although the Scriptures were given by God through those who

were a part of the community of believers, in no way can they be considered the product of the church and thus under its authority. The apostles insisted that their authority was not derived from the church, but directly from the Lord of the church. Instead of the church producing the apostles, the Bible teaches that the apostles and prophets were foundational to the church (Eph. 2:20). Thus, their inspired words are basic for belief and practice within the church. The church devotes itself to "the apostles' teaching" and not to the teaching of the church (Acts 2:42; see also Gal. 1:8). It must abide by the commands of the apostles because they spoke the Word of God (1 Cor. 14:37; 1 Thes. 2:13).

The final option for our authority is to look outside of the subjectivity of our own minds to the objective revelation of God. As we have seen in earlier chapters, the Scriptures claim to be that revelation, the inspired Word of God. As such, they claim absolute authority over all people.

Isaiah's prophecy begins with the words, "Listen, O heavens, and hear, O earth; for the Lord speaks" (1:2). When later the people refused to submit to God, choosing to follow other voices, the prophet emphatically pointed to the only authority, declaring, "To the law and to the testimony! If they do not speak according to this Word, it is because they have no dawn" (Isa. 8:20).

This same authority of the Word is evident in the warning of Jeremiah, "Cursed is the man who does not heed the words of this covenant" (11:3). Along with the many expressions of delight in the Law of God, the Psalmist declared his utmost respect for its authority: "My flesh trembles for fear of Thee, and I am afraid of Thy judgments" (Ps. 119:120).

In the New Testament the apostles also acknowledged the authority of the Old Testament Scriptures and placed their own words on an equal level (see 2 Peter 3:2). Above all Jesus, whom the church confesses as its Lord and teacher, accepted the full authority of Scripture, submitting His total life to its truth.

The implications of this respect for the Scriptures as the authoritative voice of the God of the universe are many. Nowhere are they more evident than in the life of our Lord. His mind was filled with the teaching of the Scriptures, demonstrating that He had spent much time in them, studying and meditating on their truth. He surely had the same attitude of delight and love for the

Word expressed so frequently by the Psalmist (Ps. 1:2; Ps. 119:14, 16, 47-48, 97). This recognition of the Scriptures as the authoritative voice of His heavenly Father caused Jesus to walk in perfect obedience to their instruction.

Our own experience of the Scriptures must begin with a similar acknowledgment and respect for their absolute authority. It is Almighty God who is speaking in them. Our recognition of this truth should bring great comfort and joy to us, as it did to the Psalmist. The God of the universe calls us to Himself, not only declaring His will for our lives, but promising in love and grace to enable us to walk in fellowship with Him.

This recognition of the authority of the Word, however, will also give us that healthy, awesome respect for it that we find in the psalms. Again and again we read of our obligation to *fear* the Lord. Such fear is the "beginning of wisdom" (Ps. 111-10) and "a fountain of life" (Prov. 14:27). Surely, there is no fear of the Lord which does not at the same time fear His Word.

2. *Sufficiency of the Bible*. We must not only be convinced of the authority of the Scriptures; we must also believe that their content is significant for our lives. They may be trustworthy, but do they meet our needs? Or must we turn elsewhere?

When we ask these questions we find that the Apostle Paul declared Scripture profitable to make us "adequate, equipped for every good work" (2 Tim. 3:17). Jesus Himself prohibited any addition of human thought to the written message of Scripture (Matt. 15:3, 6). It is "to the Law and to the testimony" that we are continually pointed as the answer to life (Isa. 8:20).

This claim to sufficiency, however, must be understood within the context of the purpose of the Bible. The Bible makes no claim to be a compendium of all knowledge. Obviously, there are facts of biology, for example, not found in the Scriptures. The purpose of the Scriptures is to give "the wisdom that leads to salvation" (2 Tim. 3:15). Now salvation in its comprehensive sense means that complete wholeness of life which comes from knowing God and His will and walking in the full light of this revelation. Thus, it is the knowledge of God and His direction for life that is totally sufficient in Scripture. As Matthew Henry once noted, "the Scriptures were written not to make us astronomers, but to make us saints."

Specifically, the Scriptures contain all we need to know to come to salvation and to live the Christian life. Thus, we find the Apostle Paul reasoned "from the Scriptures" as he sought to win people to Christ (Acts 17:2; 26:22). "Preach the Word," he advised young Timothy, and he exhorted him to do the work of evangelism (2 Tim. 4:2, 5). Of particular note is Jesus' answer to the man who asked for a miracle to convince his brothers of the truth: "If they do not listen to Moses and the Prophets, neither will they be persuaded if someone rises from the dead" (Luke 16:31). The Gospel is the power of God for salvation and there is no Gospel outside of that revealed in the Scriptures.

The Scriptures likewise testify to their complete sufficiency for our Christian walk. Some of the most profound statements to this effect are given by the Psalmist in the great psalm of the Word, Psalm 119. In the Word, the Psalmist found hope (v. 49; see also Rom. 15:4). The Word brought comfort and life (v. 50). It gave wisdom greater than all his enemies and insight above his teachers (vv. 98-99). Understanding comes with age, but the psalmist declared, "I understand more than the aged, because I have observed Thy precepts" (v. 100; cf. v. 104). "Thy Word is a lamp to my feet, and a light to my path" (v. 105).

While this light and understanding centers in salvation, we should not hastily separate them from other human knowledge. No realm of knowledge remains unaffected by the truth of Scripture. Someone has said, "The Bible is not only the revealer of the unknown God to man, but His grand interpreter as the God of nature. In revealing God it has given us the key that unlocks the profoundest mysteries of creation." Philosophy, history, science— every area of knowledge is illumined by the light of Scripture so that we may use it in the furtherance of God's purposes.

The Scriptures, then, are our standard. By them we know the meaning of life and how to fulfill God's purpose for our existence. Without them we only grope as blind men along life's path. With them we can walk in the light of the Lord.

Understanding God's Word

A few months ago our neighbor, knowing that I taught theology at a seminary, asked me about the Bible. He said that he listened to various preachers on television and noticed that they just picked out a verse anywhere and used it for a text. "How," he asked, "does the Bible fit together?"

To many people the Bible is a closed book because they do not understand it. It speaks in a strange language about things that happened long ago.

This is the reason the medieval church often denied ordinary people the use of the Bible. Lack of understanding, they reasoned, would only lead to confusion. The interpretation of the Scriptures was reserved for the doctors of the church.

Against this attitude the Protestant Reformers proclaimed the clarity of the Scriptures. By this they did not mean that everything in the Bible was absolutely clear. They meant that the fundamental message of Scripture was understandable to the average person. Skill in the original languages of the Bible and acquaintance with the history and culture of biblical times aid in the understanding of difficult parts, but the basic truths of salvation and our walk with the Lord may be understood by all.

This position is supported by the Scriptures themselves for they were written not to special leaders but to all people of God. Furthermore, they were to be read in the churches (Col. 4:16; Rev. 1:3). Finally, the people themselves had the responsibility to judge whether one who proclaimed the Word was true or not, and they were supposed to do this on the basis of the truth they had received (Deut. 13:1-5; Gal. 1:8-9).

A few general principles here will help us understand what God is saying in Scripture.

1. Natural Interpretation. The natural interpretation of Scripture is simply taking the language of the Bible as we would any other human language. God did not inspire the human authors to write in some kind of cryptic language. If He had, He would have had to give us the key to its understanding. The doctrine of inspiration, however, teaches that God by the Holy Spirit used ordinary human language to convey His truth.

Ordinary human language is composed of words arranged in certain grammatical relationships. We grasp the message by paying close attention to the meanings of the words and their relationships in the structure of the sentences. We get the meaning of the Bible in the same way. Furthermore, ordinary language uses words in various ways. Sometimes we understand a strictly literal sense; at other times we recognize a variety of figurative expressions including similes, metaphors, hyperbole, and parables. The biblical authors followed this same pattern and it is extremely important that we recognize these uses.

In seeking to differentiate the literal sense from the figurative, we must use all of the teaching of Scripture as well as our knowledge of the world about us. For example, when Scripture speaks of "the wings of the wind," our knowledge of the wind tells us to take wings in a figurative way. On the other hand, when Scripture refers to God riding on a cherub (2 Sam. 22:11), we must not hastily conclude that the cherub is figurative simply because we have had no experience of one.

Today, scientific rationalism leads many to quickly conclude that portions of the Bible are not actually historical because they contain events that have never occurred in human experience. The fall of man, for example, with the eating of fruit from the tree and the talking snake, or Jonah and the great fish are considered mythological stories which teach theological truth. It is difficult to see, however, how one who believes in the God of Scriptures who intervenes in His creation at His good pleasure, can summarily rule out a supernatural event just because things do not happen that way all the time.

2. *Situational Interpretation.* One of the principal aids in the correct interpretation and application of the Scriptures is some understanding of the basic structure of the Bible. It is not a book of timeless truths which God has somehow dropped from heaven into history. Rather, it is a record of God's involvement with His people in history and spans many centuries during which God guides all history to its sure goal.

God's dealings with His people changed throughout this time as His program unfolded. Thus, it is of vital importance in approaching any passage to ask, "When and to whom was this written?" For example, the Mosaic law with its many regulations was given only to Israel and, according to Scripture, came to an end with Christ (Gal. 3:24-25). While the righteous principles expressed in the Law are eternal and carry on into the New Testament church, we must not insist that the specific regulations designed for the good of Israel at a particular time in history be imposed on all peoples at all times. One may think, for example, that certain of the dietary laws are beneficial for health. But to insist that they are God's law for all time would be a serious misinterpretation.

Not only must we take into account the time and the particular people and their situation, but we must consider the culture of the people to whom the Word came. The Scriptures were written to specific people, giving them practical instructions for life in their own culture. Illustrations of this may be found in the commands to "greet all the brethren with a holy kiss" (1 Thes. 5:26) or "wash one another's feet" (John 13:14). In instances such as these, the interpreter must ask whether these actions themselves are intended as universal commands or whether they are particular cultural expressions of universal principles.

Although some Christians have held that foot-washing is to be practiced in the church, most have accepted both of these commands as instances of cultural expressions of spiritual principles. Love among brethren is the permanent principle; it was expressed in that particular culture with a kiss even as it is today in certain places. Similarly, foot-washing was an act of the servant in that day. The permanent principle is the obligation of service in any particular culture.

Some knowledge of the various customs of biblical times and a study of their relation to spiritual truth will generally provide help in sorting out the cultural expression from the permanent truth that God is speaking to us. There is no indication, for example, that the kiss was either practiced throughout Scripture or even demanded for all. Nor does Scripture explain or imply the spiritual import of that particular act.

3. *Holistic Interpretation.* Thomas Watson, the Puritan divine, pointed to another important principle for gaining an understanding of Scripture when he said, "Scripture is to be its own interpreter, or rather the Spirit speaking in it; nothing can cut the diamond but the diamond; nothing can interpret Scripture but Scripture."

Although written by various human authors over centuries of time, the Bible is a unified harmonious whole because it was at the same time authored by the one Spirit of truth. Thus, the various portions of Scripture do not exist in isolation; they are part of the whole revelation of God. As such, they must be interpreted in relation to the truth of the whole Bible. We err when we take certain statements and fail to relate them to others on the same theme.

Jesus' prohibition about judging another (Matt. 7:1), for example, must be understood in relation to the Apostle's teaching that believers are not to go to pagan courts with each other but are to settle their differences in the church (1 Cor. 6:1-2). Similarly, the truth concerning the practice of forgiveness involves the command to forgive as God has forgiven us, suggesting that we graciously forgive no matter what the other party does. But we must also consider Jesus' words, "and if he repents, forgive him" (Luke 17:3). The true interpretation of any passage comes only as we see it in relation to the whole.

Obviously, anything more than a superficial understanding of Scripture requires time and effort in study. But if we had a letter from someone we loved, even if it were written in another language, we would make every effort to understand its contents. The nature of the Bible as the Word of our God and its life-giving truth for our lives surely make it worth our effort.

Hearing the Word

The final link in applying Scripture to our lives is in our *hearing*. "God has spoken," J.I. Packer writes, "and godliness means *hearing* His Word." Hearing in the biblical sense means that we give ear to His Word, we attend to it, we learn it, and we put it into practice. Such hearing means that when we have read the promises of God and understood what they mean, we practice them. By faith we rely on their truthfulness because they are the authoritative Word of our God.

Hearing the Word of God means also that we obey its principles for every relationship of life—men and God, husbands and wives, children and parents, citizens and rulers, even actions toward enemies and friends. We are truly listening to God when these words take precedence over our immediate happiness because we trust Him who knows far better than ourselves the path of true joy.

Books For Further Reading

Custer, Steward. *Does Inspiration Demand Inerrancy?* Nutley, NJ: The Craig Press, 1968.

Gaussen, L. *The Inspiration of the Holy Scriptures.* Chicago: Moody Press, 1949.

Haley, John W. *Alleged Discrepancies of the Bible.* Andover: Warren F. Draper, 1874. (Reprinted, Baker)

Harris, R. Laird. *Inspiration and Canonicity of the Bible.* Grand Rapids: Zondervan Publishing House, 1957.

Henry, Carl F. H. ed. *Revelation and the Bible.* Grand Rapids: Baker Book House, 1967.

Lightner, Robert P. *The Saviour and the Scriptures.* Philadelphia: Presbyterian and Reformed Publishing Company, 1966.

Lindsell, Harold. *The Battle for the Bible.* Grand Rapids: Zondervan Publishing House, 1976.

Pache, Rene. *The Inspiration and Authority of Scripture.* Chicago: Moody Press, 1970.

Packer, J.I. *"Fundamentalism" and the Word of God.* Grand Rapids: Wm. B. Eerdmans Publishing Company, 1958.

Pinnock, Clark H. *Biblical Revelation.* Chicago: Moody Press, 1971.

Thomas, Thomas A. *The Doctrine of The Word of God.* Philadelphia: Presbyterian and Reformed Publishing Company, 1972.

Warfield, Benjamin B. *The Inspiration and Authority of the Bible.* Philadelphia: Presbyterian and Reformed Publishing Company, 1948.

Wenham, John W. *Christ & the Bible.* Downers Grove, Ill.: InterVarsity Press, 1973.

Young, Edward J. *Thy Word Is Truth.* Grand Rapids: Wm. B. Eerdmans Publishing Company, 1957.

This reading list, compiled by the author, is not necessarily the recommendation of the publisher.